Travels with
PEAKY
and
SPIKE

Doreen Speckmann's
Quilting Adventures

Doreen Speckmann

C&T PUBLISHING

Copyright © 1999 Doreen Speckmann

Developmental Editors: Harold Nadel, Barbara Konzak Kuhn
Technical Editor: Sara Kate MacFarland
Cover Design: Kristen Yenche
Book Design: Kristen Yenche
Illustrations: Kandy Petersen
Original Peaky and Spike illustration by Mary Jo Scandin
Variations on Peaky and Spike by Norman Remer

Attention Teachers: C&T Publishing, Inc. encourages you to use
this book as a text for teaching. Contact us at 800-284-1114 or
www.ctpub.com for more information about the C&T Teachers
Program.

Library of Congress Cataloging-in-Publication Data
Speckmann, Doreen, 1950-1999
    Travels with Peaky and Spike : Doreen Speckmann's quilting
adventures / Doreen Speckmann.
    p. cm.
  Includes index.
  ISBN 1-57120-076-2 (paper trade)
  1. Patchwork Patterns. 2. Quilting Patterns. 1. Title.
  TT835 .S648 1999
  746.46'041--dc21
                                    99-6315
                                    CIP

Published by C&T Publishing, Inc.
P.O. Box 1456
Lafayette, California 94549

Printed in Hong Kong

10 9 8 7 6 5 4 3 2

Contents

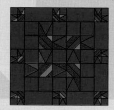

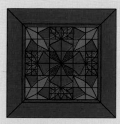

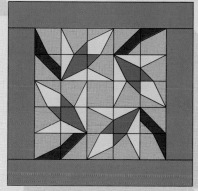

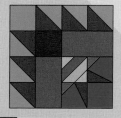

Introduction

Almost 10 years ago, I got a call from George Schy of A-1 Tours in Clearwater, Florida. He was going into the specialty travel business with his son and was wondering if I would be interested in going on a quilting cruise. I've always lived in Wisconsin, where the winters can weigh heavily indeed, so the decision was easy. Thus began my quilting life on the high seas.

For those of you who are accustomed to seeing my face in the ads in the quilting magazines, you might be fooled into thinking that I have always lived a life of travel and adventure. Not so. I'm the oldest of six children. David and Doris Punzel created Doreen, Dwight, Dennis, Debbie, Diana and Doug (way too cute) and they had the good sense to not take us all that far from home. This was before the era of the minivan so there weren't enough seats by the window. When they could afford a real vacation (not staying with relatives), they rented a fishing cabin in northern Wisconsin. Though he won't admit it, I'm sure my father called ahead to be sure that there were at least 500 spiders in the outhouse. We tried camping, and occasionally actually had a good time. We had nothing so posh as a camper, and life got distinctly better when we learned not to pitch the tent at the bottom of a hill without a

ground cloth or trench. I remember being damp a lot. The fantasy of leaving the state was exciting; visiting another country would have been unimaginable.

So, the thought of going on an international cruise was very exciting indeed. I worried that no one would be interested in going on a quilting cruise. I worried about my inadequate wardrobe. I worried about what I was going to teach and whether anyone would like what I planned—when I figured out what that would be. I worried a lot. But everything turned out well in spite of the beginning of the Gulf War during the first cruise. What I discovered was that there were quite a few quilters who were looking for an excuse to go cruising. It is a wonderful vacation for anyone, but especially for women. Someone else cleans your room, serves your food, turns down your bed, and artfully arranges your nightie on the bed, with a chocolate on the pillow. (It always takes the staff a few days to figure out that the Mickey Mouse t-shirt is my negligee.) And of course it is wonderful to leave winter behind to frolic in sun and sea. I mastered the basics of snorkeling and learned how to enjoy the sun without turning as red as a lobster.

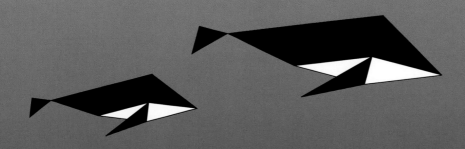

One of the most frequent questions I get asked is, "When is there time to quilt with so many meals and cruise activities?" We choose cruises that offer at least three days at sea.

You can only spend a few hours in the hot tropical sun without inviting a smorgasbord of disasters. And after a round or two of napkin folding and vegetable carving demonstrations, you find that a chance to play with fabric and sit at a sewing machine is a welcome relief. We run our classes just like a land-bound conference, from 9 to noon and 1 to 4pm. I don't do this all by myself. Over the years I have been joined by some of the best teachers in the country...Judi Warren, Gwen Marston, Joe Cunningham, Faye Anderson, Ruth McDowell, Katie Pasquini, Blanche Young, Liz Porter, Judy Dales, Anita Murphy, Mary Stori, Jean Wells, and Catherine Anthony. We had an international cruise and were joined by Deirdre Amsden from England and Greta Moe from Norway. My method for choosing a teacher is to think about who I would like to spend a week with and it has worked quite well.

One of our biggest treats in the years that the ship stops in Nassau is attending a quilt show put on by the Stepping Stones Quilt Guild. Maria Chisnall, a Bahamian quilter, was on our first cruise; she arranged to have our group met at the ship and led to their quilt show. It was glorious! We were amazed by the brilliant colors they used with such expertise and that they bothered to make quilts at all. It was so warm, even during their "winter," that warm bed covers didn't seem like a priority. It reinforced what I guess we have always known; making quilts has more to do with playing with fabric and enjoying the company of other creative souls than it has to do with keeping warm. We were also able to find a fabric store within blocks of the ship. Maria introduced us to Androsia fabric, batik made on Andros, another Bahamian island, with images of turtles, dolphins, sharks, lobsters, and hibiscus.

Going on a cruise is a wonderful luxury and I feel privileged to be able to go. But if cruising isn't in your plans for the near future, here's your chance to go on a virtual cruise. Welcome aboard and enjoy the quilts.

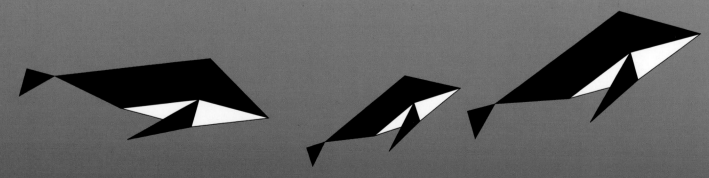

The Story of Peaky & Spike

In my early days of quiltmaking, when books were scarce, I fell in love with a Storm at Sea quilt in Margaret Ickis's *The Standard Book of Quiltmaking*. But there weren't enough instructions for this beginning quiltmaker to feel sufficiently confident to tackle it. Then in 1980, I discovered Beth and Jeff Gutcheon's *The Quilt Design Workbook* with their quilt "Judy in Arabia" on the front cover, and I was ready. I could see that the isosceles triangle, squared off with two right triangles having one leg twice the length of the other, gave whatever quilt it was in the illusion of curves. I started using this unit, and eventually I dubbed it Peaky and Spike.

I knew in my head which piece was which, but I always referred to them as a pair. It surprised me when students would mix up which piece was Peaky and which was Spike. Finally, in Denver, my students explained that the large triangle must be Peaky because it looked like a mountain peak and the skinny triangle had to be Spike because it looked like a railroad spike. I recognized the logic of this, but my envisioning of Peaky and Spike had been drastically different.

I drew them for the first time there in Denver, and they have changed very little since then. If one of them was going to be a girl, it definitely had to be the one with the big brain and little butt. Spike is his own man—enough said.

And they have taken on a life of their own. They have traveled with me in spirit for years until 1996, when they became real with a little help from my husband, Pete. Since then they have been to Hawaii, France, Australia, New Zealand, Alaska, and Great Britain. I'm now known not only as a quiltmaker and teacher, but also as the Mother of Peaky and Spike. Although Peaky and Spike don't appear in all my quilts, they do show up very frequently. They are part of a whole family of units from which you can make some extremely interesting quilts.

Quilt Basics

Before I tell you how to make the quilts in this book, I want to discuss quilt design. My hope is that, when you understand how easily things go together, you will feel free to make changes and put your own personal stamp on my ideas. That's what quiltmakers have done for as long as quilts have been made.

I love traditional quilts. When I started making quilts, I was sure there were enough traditional designs to keep me busy well into my old age. What I should have known then was that I'm not capable by temperament of doing what I'm supposed to do. Give me a rule and my first response is: "Why?" The second question follows automatically: "What will happen to me if I don't?" I quickly discovered that blocks could be changed by taking parts of one block and putting them into another. I might change the direction of a unit, expand a block by adding units, or take away or add lines.

My first quilts were constructed of very simple divisions of the square—the square, half-square triangle, rectangles, quarter-square triangles, and a four-patch.

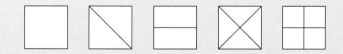

I could make quite a few blocks with just these units.

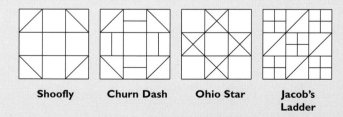

Shoofly   **Churn Dash**   **Ohio Star**   **Jacob's Ladder**

After mastering these, I experimented a little and added more units to my repertoire—the skinny triangles that make the Storm at Sea stormy, the trapezoid that turns an Ohio Star into Night and Noon, the Flying Geese unit, and a square on point.

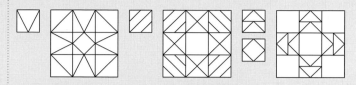

Along the way, the units got names. The first ones were easy to describe geometrically: half-square and quarter-square triangles, four-patch. But units I added later were harder to describe easily with geometric terms. I made up names that made some kind of sense to me: I saw Peaky and Spike.

New units kept growing from old. By taking away one side of the empty Ice Cream Cone, I had a new unit called Mutt and Jeff.

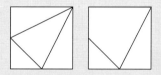

This is the unit that I used in *Antigua* (page 32), and in the Lily blocks in the Cruise Quilts and the Little Star blocks in the Alaska quilts.

By splitting a full Ice Cream Cone in half, I found Sliver. I turned Sliver into a pectoral fin on the humpback whale.

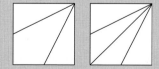

Here's a quick peek at all the units you use for the quilts in the book.

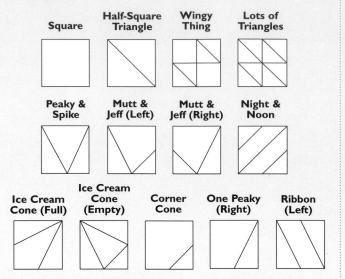

There are some oddball pieces used in the Whale blocks, Long Fish blocks, and *Nightblooms in Nassau,* and they are noted in the specific quilt instructions and in the template section.

Yardage Schmardage

Now is a good time to discuss yardage. I have done my best to give you accurate and generous yardage for all the quilts, because that is the responsible approach in a quiltmaking book. But, for most of my quiltmaking life, I've been indifferent to yardage. If I bought 1 yard of fabric, I would need 1 1/2 yards. So I bought 4 yards and needed 4 1/2 yards. Running out of fabric became commonplace, and finding substitutes quite exciting. Some people climb mountains; I start quilts without knowing if I have enough fabric to finish.

One of the realities of my quiltmaking and fabric selection is that my original choices generally don't work out. So, even if I carefully worked out the yardages and collected all my fabric in the right amounts, I would have to scramble for substitutes for one or more of them before I finished.

My favorite solution to the problem of running out of fabric is never to put myself in that position. If a design calls for turquoise, I collect lots of turquoises that vary slightly in color and texture but blend well. If I run out of

one or two of twenty prints, no one will notice a substitution. Using lots of fabrics isn't just a coping mechanism; I think it creates a richer quilt surface. When you start making quilts this way, you will buy fabric accordingly. When faced with ten great yellow fabrics at a quilt shop, I don't have to decide which one and how much to buy; I buy a half-yard of each.

We are clever women who have figured out how to solve all kinds of problems, such as buying groceries and fabric, or making time to quilt in a very busy life. Coping with a fabric shortage pales in comparison.

Cutting the Quilt

The construction of each quilt project in this book is broken down into blocks, units, and templates. Cutting instructions tell how many of each shape to cut from each fabric. I never cut the whole quilt out at once (more about this later). But, if you like what you see in the photograph and are certain about your fabric choices, you can cut everything out and hope for the best.

Tried and True

Call me old-fashioned or stubborn (or both), but I still trace around my templates and cut with scissors. To do this, first press your fabric right sides together. Place the template on the fabric, aligning the indicated grain lines to the grain of your fabric and trace with a sharp marking device—a mechanical pencil with a soft lead, or whatever shows up on the fabric, with a point sharp enough to mark right next to the edge of the template. Butt the template up to previously drawn lines and continue until you have the number of pieces you need.

Then cut. Your goal is to cut fabric pieces the same size as the templates—neither bigger nor smaller. Cutting doubled fabric speeds the process: you get two pieces for each one traced, and many of the pieces used in my quilts are reversing shapes.

Most of the time you may need both right-facing and left-facing pieces, as noted in the instructions. By cutting double, you automatically get rights and lefts. Special note is made if the template must be used on a single layer of fabric, cut one way only.

Rotary Cutting

I didn't just fall off the turnip truck. I've taught enough around the country to know that many of you wield your rotary cutter like a surgeon's knives. Of course, you can cut your fabric with a rotary cutter. But first think about what rotary cutters do best—they cut strips and make straight cuts. What they do poorly is cut around thin templates. If you are making one of the big quilts and need lots of a shape from the same fabric, cut a strip of fabric the height of the template.

Cut height of Spike

Use your template to mark the other lines,

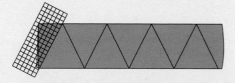

and then use a small acrylic ruler and cutter to cut on the pencil lines.

If you are making a smaller quilt and only need, for example, eight Gs, four As, and two Js, trace around the templates as you would for scissors cutting.

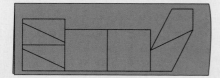

But, instead of using scissors, use an acrylic ruler to cut pieces free from a larger piece of fabric, then cut on the pencil lines.

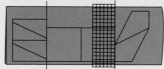

This way you can maintain accuracy while working with the tool with which you feel more comfortable. When you have cut enough pieces to see what you have, go on to the next step.

Lay Out the Pieces and Look

It's an important part of my quiltmaking process to lay out the whole quilt on my design wall. There I can see if what I have planned really works. My quilts seem to evolve from my initial plans and fabric choices. You are seeing the finished quilt and adjusted line drawings, and you could too easily assume that these were my original ideas. Yet, every quilt I've made that I like has changed somehow. Sometimes those changes were painful, especially when I had to discard a fabric that I started with. But it is this part of the process that keeps me interested in making quilts. Some people like solving crossword puzzles. What fun would that be if they printed the answers right above the puzzle? You could fill out a very neat puzzle in ink, but the challenge would be gone. If I have all the answers to the quilt before I start, it's no fun.

I assume that some of you reading this book will be happy to make the quilts as pictured, trying hard to match my fabric choices. It's nice to know when you start what the quilt will look like. You will also get acquainted with the units and piecing techniques. But once you get the hang of it, I'm sure that you will want to change the designs to suit your needs and tastes and inspirations. You might want to change the size, or the whole color concept of the quilt. The secret to making a wonderful quilt is never sew it together until you really like it. My only regret is that I won't get to see what you have done to improve on my ideas. (But, I'd be delighted to have you send photos to me at C&T Publishing.)

DESIGN WALL IDEAS

Permanent installation of a design wall in your sewing space is ideal. I put one up years ago, and I would hate to make a quilt without it. We first nailed firring strips to our plaster walls, then we nailed sound-deadening board to the firring strips. (This way we didn't have to find studs.) Sound-deadening boards look like bulletin-board material and work well when you need to pin things up. But single cut pieces don't need to be pinned if you cover the board with a fuzzy fabric. I've had good luck with felt, fleece by the yard, and cotton batting. Right now I'm using the flannel with printed grid, because I can easily keep things lined up on it.

If you don't have a wall to spare, there are other options. The cheapest is a flannel-backed vinyl tablecloth taped or pinned to the wall. The price is right, but you'll have difficulty pinning up borders on it, and its holding power decreases with the weight of the finished top.

A semi-permanent alternative can be put up when you need it and stored when not in use. Cover 2' x 4' sections of foam core with fuzzy fabric. Pull fabric tightly over the foam core and tape it to the back side; then link sections with the handywoman's best friend, duct tape. With a few nails close to the ceiling and bulldog clamps as hangers, you can put up as much design wall as you need. When you are finished, the foam core sections can be folded up and stored under a bed or at the back of a closet.

Sewing the Pieces Together

All you need for accurate machine piecing is a sewing machine that sews a perfect lock stitch and goes forward. Get out your manual and follow the manufacturer's instructions for cleaning and oiling. It's amazing how well even the humblest of sewing machines will work with a little loving care. Of course, it is fun to have a sewing machine with all the bells and whistles—built-in walking foot, needle threader, hundreds of special stitches. Change the needle often; don't wait until you hear the "pop-pop-pop" that tells you the needle is dull. I generally use a Schmetz® 80-12 needle. I work with 100% cotton thread (Star®) that is found on a cardboard tube (1200 yards). Choose a thread color that blends well with your fabric. A medium to dark gray works well with dark, cool colors, and a medium to dark beige with warm colors. Use white or off-white only when piecing light fabrics. What you are trying to avoid is stitches peeking out at the seams. Set the stitch length to 15 stitches per inch (2 on a European machine). Longer stitches may be easier to "un-sew" but the shorter stitch makes a better seam with no gaps and it will not ravel during pressing.

The next critical element for precision piecing is to sew an accurate 1/4" seam allowance, the same seam allowance that has been added to your templates. That may be the same 1/4" as your 1/4" presser foot, but not necessarily so. To be sure, place one of your templates under the presser foot and lower the needle to the sewing line. Place a small stack of Post-It® notes on the sewing machine, lined up with the right side of the template and clear of the feed dogs.

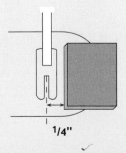

1/4"

This is a very important step, so do it carefully. Sew a few test seams and measure the seam and the size of the piece. If this sounds a bit tedious, compare it with ripping or fiddling with pieces that don't fit. It's well worth the effort.

Now you are ready to start putting your quilt together. Everyone organizes her sewing differently, so work in a way that is comfortable for you. I take "like" units in groups and chain piece (sew one step without breaking the thread between stages). Refer to the specific tips for each family of pieced units.

Piecing with Peaky and Spike

One pass: This technique joins pieces that are not identical in shape, but have no crossovers: When you are joining two pieces and you want a straight edge, line up the pieces so the little "mouse ears" hang out evenly. Start and stop stitching in the crevices.

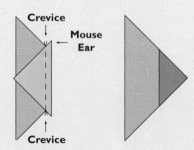

Two passes: The next group that operates under the same rules still has 45° angles. The pieces cross over each other, making one or more interior points. The rules change a little at the points. We'll use the Center Diamond as the first example.

a. Line up the triangles on opposite sides of the square; "mouse ears" should hang out evenly. Notice when you take the 1/4" seam that it does not start at the crevice. I wanted it to, but it's not right. You should be able to see a few stitches on the triangle before you hit the square.

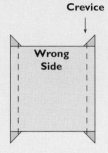

b. Press the seams away from the center.

c. Attach the other two triangles. Again the "mouse ears" will hang out evenly. This time sew from crevice to crevice. You know you've done it right when the edges are straight and the points are 1/4" from the edge. Trim away the ears. When possible, press away from the square. Being able to see the "crossroads" is important when assembling units into blocks; they are the guide-posts to the point on the right side.

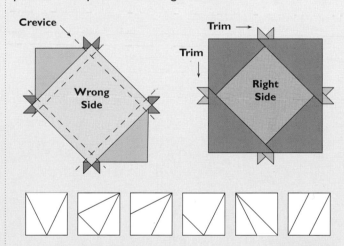

Weird angles: Now we come to the weird ones. I couldn't find any rules that applied, so for years I sewed them and just hoped for the best. I could have solved the problem by drawing in the seam line and pinning from point to point, duplicating the traditional hand piecing technique. Another alternative is to punch holes at the seam-line

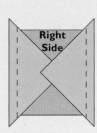

corners. Even when using an $1/8"$ paper punch, I found the holes too big and the results were only slightly better than the "happy accident" method. What I really needed was some guidelines on how to line up the two pieces. The solution is to go directly to the templates. Hold them up to the light and match the seam lines. Tape them together. Look at this to see what is happening at each end of the seam.

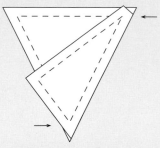

Pick up the fabric and make it look like the templates.

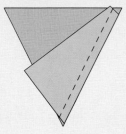

Using Peaky and Spike as an example, sew from the upper right to the center.

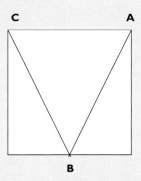

To sew the second Peaky, lay it on top of the first Peaky. Spike is taller behind the twin peaks.

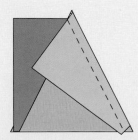 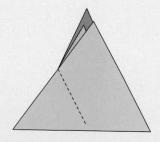

Here is what Peaky and Spike should look like finished.

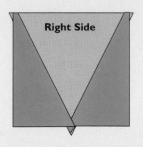 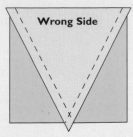

Ice Cream Cones: Here's another odd angle. Make a mock-up with templates to get your bearings. Note that you start sewing at the crevice. Sew the first Peaky onto the cone. Press away from the cone. Sew the second Peaky onto the cone. Start at the end opposite from the point in the crevice.

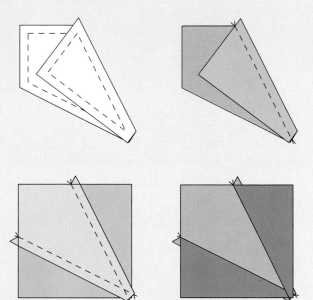

When all of the units are sewn together, pressed, and the "mouse ears" have been trimmed off, you are ready to assemble the quilt. Each quilt presents its own logical path. Often we follow the traditional route, assembling units into blocks and then sewing block to block or blocks to sashings. But there are times when you may assemble rows of units. Make a plan and follow it. Whatever path you choose, continue to press consistently and, whenever possible, oppose the seams to reduce bulk at the seam crossovers.

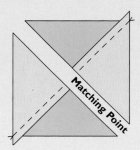

Consistent pressing will give you a flat top and make it easier to quilt. The best advice I can give you is keep looking at the piece, checking to see that nothing is turned around. Better to catch those mistakes early, instead of after the borders are on! (That slip-up can make me cranky for days.)

Helpful Hint: There is a very low-tech method for matching points perfectly. The problem arises when you have two points that have to match but you can see only the side facing you as you put it through the sewing machine.

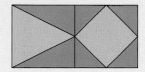

To get that perfect match, line up the units at the corners. Now peel back the seam allowances to reveal the points that need to match. With fingertips and eyeballs, match these points perfectly. Hold tightly to this spot until you wiggle a pin in just to the left of the crossroads.

Then sew the unit together with a 1/4" seam allowance, but aim to stitch across the crossroads even when the seam allowance may vary slightly.

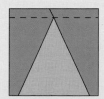

When you sew rows of units together, you may find that important crossroads fall on both sides of the rows.

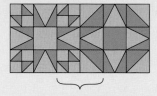

You will be able to see those crossroads only on top as you feed the fabric through the sewing machine. To solve the problem, sew partial seams. Line up and pin the units together, then sew a partial seam which intersects the visible crossroads.

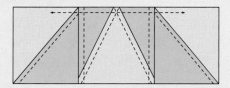

Flip the rows over and finish the seam, intersecting the crossroads that now appear. Overlap the partial seams by at least two stitches. I've given you one example of this but it may come up in a number of different ways. The essential message here is to first use your eyes and fingertips to make your matches. Secondly, if you can't see the match, consider sewing on both sides of the seam.

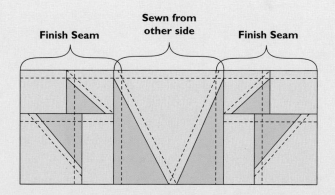

Finish Seam   **Sewn from other side**   **Finish Seam**

Pressing

Pressing is another essential element of precision piecing. The units will lie flat and be the size they are supposed to be, and the blocks will go together easily if pressed well. The benefits of good pressing continue through to the quilting.

Common quilting wisdom has maintained, "Don't use steam." Steam supposedly distorts the pieces. Another bit of quilt lore is, "Never move the iron." You are supposed to just press down with a dry iron. Fiddlesticks and tommyrot! I use steam, and I move the iron. When you steam and move, the seams are flatter with no little tucks. However, do be careful not to fan the bias edges. One of my students noticed that I press with the grain, a maneuver that may keep distortion to a minimum.

The first real rule (but not the last) in pressing is to press toward the darker fabric. Snip the "chained" pieces apart and stack them so the seam allowance is on the left and the darker fabric on top. Press from the right side, flipping the darker fabric over. The iron will move and flatten the seam. If you're left-handed, reverse these directions.

Some units require a deviation from the "always toward the darker fabric" rule. Any unit with seams that cross over each other—Flying Geese, Peaky and Spike, Ice Cream Cones, Sliver, Mutt and Jeff—should be pressed away from the center piece. If you were to press seams toward the Ice Cream Cone, for example, you would have a big wad of  fabric at the pointy end. When you press away from the cone, the piece will lie flat and you will be able to see where the seams cross and where the point is.

Seams open? This is the latest controversy in the quilt world. I will continue to be a "seams-to-one-sider," but you should experiment with both methods. Some say their quilts are even flatter and easier to quilt with the open method. The "one-siders" are convinced that an open seam is weaker. Make your own decision.

Fabric Always Makes the Quilt

You can choose an interesting pattern, construct your quilt perfectly, and still end up with a quilt that bores you thoroughly. The universal truth of quiltmaking is: Fabric makes the quilt. It sets the mood, makes design elements pop out or recede, matches room decor, reminds you of good times or a special place and, at its best, does all these at once. Each quilt has its own reason for being made. Sometimes I make a quilt with a very specific placement in mind, so the fabric is chosen to fit with what is going on in that particular room. But, these days, my walls are full and my beds are covered; I make quilts because I love to play with fabric. Because I've been places and seen things I never imagined this girl from Wisconsin would experience, I've wanted to capture the essence of these places in my quilts.

The Cruise Quilts are inspired by the brilliant turquoise water which I thought had to be retouched on the postcards—water couldn't possibly look like that (it does)—and the colorful flowers that are in bloom when everything is gray in Wisconsin. I had seen colorful fish in the salt-water tanks at pet stores, but they hadn't seemed real to me until I was swimming with them. These too had to be a part of my cruise quilts. And I didn't really have to buy fabric in the Caribbean to get these colors. It's all available in our quilt shops.

A big question you could be asking if you don't feel like redecorating your house in the Midwest to look like a cabana in Cozumel is, what do you do with these quilts after you've made them? I'm at peace with making a quilt just because I feel like it, then putting it in the closet when I'm done. But, these can make wonderful children's quilts. Or, you could plan a house party in the middle of February and get the quilts out to chase away the wintertime blues. Turn up the heat for a few hours, slice up a fresh pineapple and put some reggae music on the stereo. This can do amazing things for your attitude.

If you don't relate to the hot colors of the Caribbean, you could put your own mark on the lily quilts by coloring them a little more subtly. Soften the flowers and mellow the background for a quilt that could fit in anywhere. I can't imagine the fish any way but bright, but you may have some ideas for toning them down.

My approach to the fabric selection for the Alaskan quilts was similar. I wanted to capture the feeling of frigid waters, snow-topped mountains, evergreen trees and crystal-clear skies. So, I looked for fabric that was cool. The coolest color is blue, and I was even able to find blue fabrics with overprinted snowflakes. It's amazing what you will find in the marketplace once you get an inspiration. Since I started making Alaskan quilts, various fabric companies have produced fabrics with orcas, humpback whales, snowflakes, North American wildlife, grizzly bears, bush planes, and glaciers. We all understand that fabric designs are here today and gone tomorrow, but I'm certain there will be some special fabrics out there when you start to look.

The problem with working with so many blues, greens, and grays is keeping everything from mushing together. So, make sure that the background blue behind the Pine Trees and Sitka Spruce is light enough to let the tree triangle stand out. Work with the whale fabrics so you don't lose the whales in the water. How much contrast is enough? There's no efficient way for me to answer that. There is no magic for putting fabrics together except to look at your choices and make changes when the result isn't exactly right. This sounds easy, but it can be the hardest part. I have struggled with many a quilt because I was too stubborn to admit that my initial choices weren't working. The more you sew together, the less likely you will be to make changes or toss away a bad fabric choice. I try to avoid this problem by putting everything up on a design wall before I sew. If I'm not sure about a series of choices, I let them marinate on the wall for a couple of days. A bad choice will look worse after three days, and a good choice will look better. All of this may sound a little airy, especially if you are looking for cold, hard facts about fabric combining. If quilting were an exact science it wouldn't be as much fun and I wouldn't be doing it.

St. Thomas 28" x 28"
Machine pieced and quilted
by the author

St. Maarten 24" x 24"
Machine pieced and quilted
by the author

St. Thomas: Spinning Fish
St. Maarten: Spinning Lilies

There seems to be no end to how many ways you can turn the Fish or Lily blocks. In these quilts, I spun the motifs around a center square. The result is a Five-Patch block that could be a wallhanging or the start of a bigger quilt. And I didn't have to travel to the tropics for the fabrics that make these quilts sing. The fabrics for the Fish blocks and for the background and border of the Lilies are Marimekko® from Finland (not exactly a tropical paradise). I didn't even have to travel to Finland to buy them; I found them at a housewares outlet in Berkeley, California—pulled them out of a barrel and paid by the pound. Though quilt shops are our best fabric resource, keep your eyes open for the fabric treasures that are hiding where you least expect them.

Spinning Fish

✷ Units

Large Fish

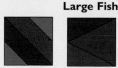

Little Fish

✷ Templates

Yardage Schmardage

Assorted Blue Prints for Background: 3/8 yard total

Assorted Prints (Oranges, Yellows, Pinks, Blues, and Greens) for Fish Bodies: 1/2 yard total

Fabrics

There are four Large Fish and eight Little Fish. I had a geometrically patterned fabric that was so unusual I could cut almost the whole fish from one piece. What looks like intricate piecing is really just careful cutting of a really neat fabric.

✷ Cutting Instructions

Fabric	Template	Total
Background	L4	8
	G4 (left and right)	16
	A4	4
	4 1/2" x 8 1/2" strips	4
Border	B2	8
	L2	16
	4 1/2" x 8 1/2" strips	8
Fish Fabrics	D2	8
	F4	8
	L4	16
	D1	16
	F2	16
	G2 (left and right)	32

Sew all units together. Then assemble fish sections. Use short seam technique (page 34) to sew fish border sections to center square.

Spinning Lilies

NOTE: The following instructions are for St. Maarten.

☀ Units

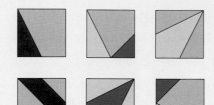

☀ Templates

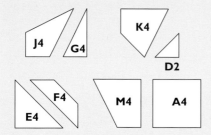

Yardage Schmardage

Floral Print for Background:
  1/2 yard total
Dark Green: 1/4 yard total
Assorted Pinks: 3/8 yard total
Border: 7/8 yard

Fabrics

Mix up the pink fabrics by cutting enough pieces of each from four different prints. These pinks are strong enough to support a busy background. Although the border looks pieced, it is not! The fabric is printed in different colored squares.

☀ Cutting Instructions

Fabric	Template	Total
Four pinks (of each, cut)		
	J4	8
	G4 (left and right)	16
	D2	8
Dark Green	F4	4
	G4 (left only)	4
Background	A4	1
	M4 (right only)	4
	D2	4
	E4	4
	K4 (left and right)	8
	G4 (left and right)	8

Sew all units together. Then assemble lily and leaf sections. Join a leaf section to each lily. Use short seam technique (page 34) to sew lilies and leaves to center square.

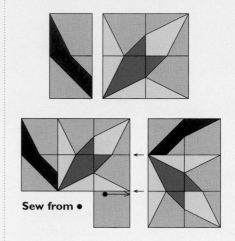

Sew from ●

Add border, 4" (finished) to complete the quilts.

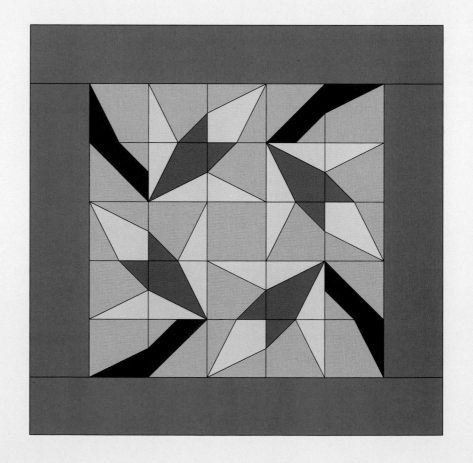

Jamaica: Concentric Fish

Jamaica 32" x 32"

Machine pieced by the author and machine quilted by Gayle Wallace

Jamaica: Concentric Fish

Just when I thought I had done all that could be done with fish, I fooled around on graph paper and came up with this design. I like the concentric circles created by the fins, which also give me a great place to vary the backgrounds. The center looked clunky until I added the Little Fish blocks, creating another circle.

Concentric Fish

Units

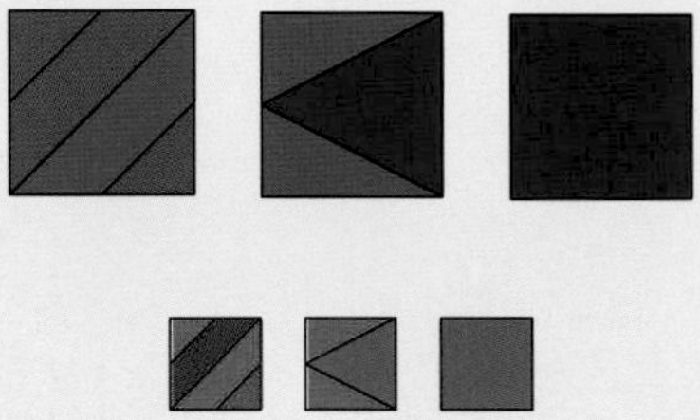

Templates

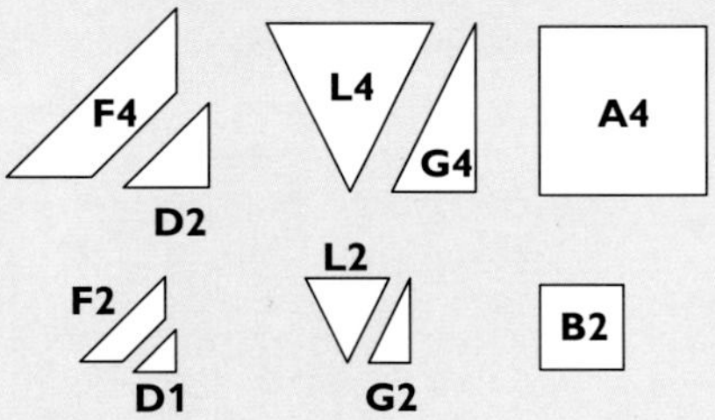

Yardage Schmardage

Assorted Turquoise to Teal Prints for Background: 5/8 yard total

Assorted Prints (Pinks, Oranges, and Yellows) for Fish: 7/8 yard total

Border Fabric: 1 1/8 yard total

Fabrics

I used three different turquoise to teal prints for the background, grading from medium to dark. For the fish I chose fabrics that are bright and would show up well against the backgrounds. This quilt is made using three pinks, four oranges, and four yellows. The border fabric has it all: the teals, a little orange, a little pink, and a little yellow. You may want to choose your border first and work from there.

Cutting Instructions

Fabric	Template	Total
Yellows	D1	8
	F2	8
	G2	16
Orange	D2	8
	F4	8
	G4	16
Pink	D2	8
	F4	8
	G4	16
Teal 1(light)	L2	8
	B2	4
Teal 2 (med)	L4	8
Teal 3 (dark)	L4	8
	A4	8

Assemble the units, starting at the Night and Noons, and then Peaky and Spikes. Sew four Little Fish together, following the illustration. Repeat construction for outside row of pink fish.

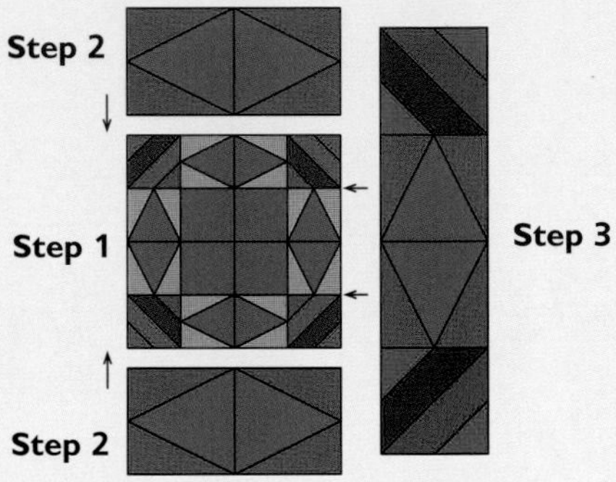

Top measures 24" square before adding borders. Add the border, 6" (finished), to complete the quilt.

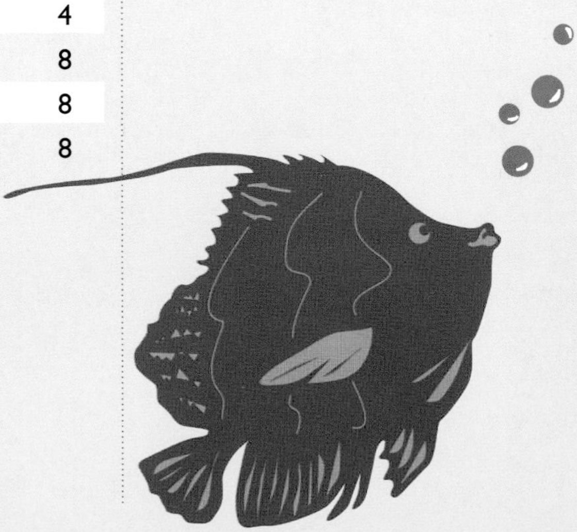

IT'S ELECTRIC!

"There's a dancing fool" may not be the first words that come to mind when you think of Doreen Speckmann ...if indeed you had ever thought of me at all. But when the music starts, my feet need to move. On our first cruise, Callie Chisnall (daughter of my Bahamian friend Maria) taught my daughter Megan to do the Electric Slide. It's the grandmother of all line dances, to a Caribbean beat. I had a whole year to practice and was ready by the next cruise to teach and lead not only quilting but synchronized dance movements. A few fearless souls joined in, and soon we filled the dance floor with what I proudly call "The Quilters' Dance and Drill Team." It's become a tradition now, and I've heard the watchers have almost as much fun as the dancers—though I'll never understand that.

Grand Cayman 34" x 34"

Machine pieced and quilted by the author

The design is basically the same as the concentric fish of *Jamaica* fame, but the mini Lily blocks didn't fit in the center. With this arrangement, they look really great toward the border.

Concentric Lilies

☼ Units

☼ Templates

Yardage Schmardage

Blue for Center Background and Outer Border: 1 1/8 yards

Blue for Outer Background: 7/8 yard

Orange Prints: 3/8 yard total

Pink Prints: 3/8 yard total

Yellow Prints: 1/4 yard total

Fabrics

I used two background fabrics: the center circle matches the border fabric. A strip of the second background surrounds the pieced part of the quilt to float the lilies at the border's edge. Choose any floral colors that show up on the background fabric. I used colors that remind me of the Caribbean: pinks, oranges, and yellows.

☼ Cutting Instructions

Fabric	Template	Total
Background (center)		
	K4 (left and right)	8
	G4 (left and right)	8
Background (outer)		
	K4 (left and right)	8
	K2 (left and right)	16
	G2 (left and right)	16
Orange	J4	4
	D2	8
	G4 (left and right)	16
Pink	J4	8
	D2	8
	G4 (left and right)	16
Yellow	J2	16
	D1	16
	G2 (left and right)	32

Assemble the units. The center of the quilt should measure 24" square. Add at least an inch of the outside background to all four sides. Add borders, 1" (finished) and 4" (finished), mitering the corners, to complete the quilt.

Long Fish 31 1/2" x 31 1/2"

Machine pieced by the author and machine quilted by Gayle Wallace

Long Fish

I was fiddling around on graph paper and came up with yet another fish, this time created from two Peaky and Spikes with a Flying Goose for the tail.

To add interest, I used two different sizes of fish. However, the fish didn't come alive, though, until I added beads for eyes.

Long Fish

☀ Blocks

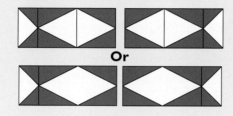

Or

☀ Units

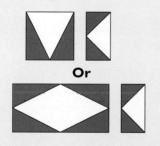

Or

☀ Templates

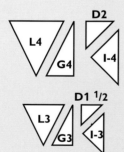

Or

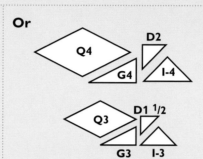

One 6 1/2" square for center
(6" finished)

One 1 1/2" strip for purple borders
(1" finished)

Yardage Schmardage

Teal to Purple Print for Center Background and Outside Border
3" (finished): 1 1/8 yards total

Teal tone-on-tone for Outer Background: 1/4 yard total

Purple Stripe for Inner Borders
1" (finished): 3/4 yard total

Black and White Print for Fish:
1/2 yard total

Fabrics

I was interested to see how this black-and-white fabric would look when cut, so I used the same fabric for all the fish. They each could have been different fabrics. The background fabric in the center square of the fish is the same fabric used for the border.

☀ Cutting Instructions

Fabric	Template	Total
Center Background		
	G4 (left and right)	16
	D2	8
	6 1/2" square	1
Outer Background		
	G3 (left and right)	32
	D1 1/2	16
	2" x 3 1/2" strips	4
	1 1/2" x 3 1/2" strips	8
Black and white	L4	8
	I-4	4
	L3	16
	I-3	8

Assemble all the fish first. Use the "short seam" technique (page 34) to sew the bigger fish to the center square. Add borders to center section, then add smaller fish. Add the border to complete the quilt.

Playa del Carmen 28" x 28"

Machine pieced by the author and machine quilted by Gayle Wallace

Playa del Carmen: All the Fish

My goal here was to put all the fish, both the original Little Fish and the Long Fish blocks, into one quilt.

I'm not even sure you can tell they are fish, but I liked the design and the opportunity to use really wild fabric.

All the Fish

☀ Units

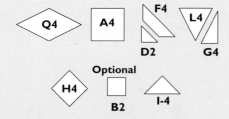

☀ Templates

Yardage Schmardage

Turquoise 1 for Center Background:
$3/8$ yard total

Turquoise 2 for Outer Border:
$3/8$ yard total

Yellow/Orange Check: $1/8$ yard total

Yellow/Orange Spotted Print:
$3/8$ yard total

Orange/Yellow Swirly Print:
$1/2$ yard total

Paisley Print: $1/4$ yard total

Shaded Orange Print: $1/4$ yard total

Purple/Orange Check: $1/4$ yard total

Fabrics

Obviously I was not trying for subtle and tasteful when choosing colors for this small piece, so I assembled a group of seven fabrics based on yellow and orange or orange and red. The Long Fish fabric with its four ribbons of turquoise is ideal in this design. I found this fabric in Australia (a Jimmy Pike design). The two turquoise blues cool things down so you can stand to look at the quilt. I think the overall design would be just as effective using softer colors.

☀ Cutting Instructions

Fabric	Templates	Total
Turquoise 1 (Center Background)		
	A4	4
	L4	8
	G4 (left and right)	8
Turquoise 2 (Outer Border)		
	G4 (left and right)	32
	D2	28
Yellow/Orange Check		
	D2	8
Yellow/Orange Spotted Print		
	L4	4
	G4 (left and right)	8
	D2	16
Orange/Yellow Swirly Print		
	Q4	8
	I-4	8
Paisley Print	L4	4
	H4	1
	G4 (left and right)	8
Shaded Orange Print		
	F4	4
	G4 (left and right)	8
Purple/Orange Check		
	D2	8
	F4	4

Assemble all the units. Join them as shown in the illustration, to complete the quilt.

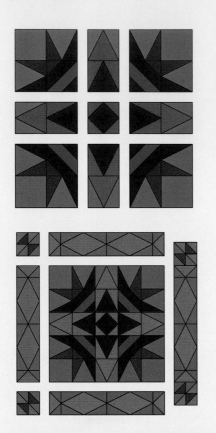

Cozumel: Fish on Point

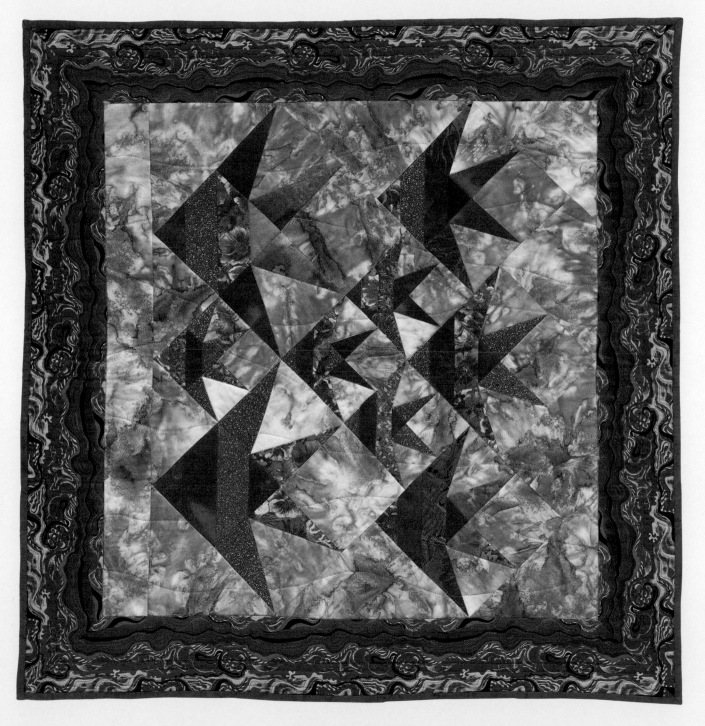

Cozumel 30" x 31"
Machine pieced by the author and machine quilted by Gayle Wallace

Cozumel: Fish on Point

I designed this quilt for the Caribbean Cruise in 1996. The challenge was to use three different sizes of fish and figure out how to put everything together. The "short seam" technique (page 34) worked perfectly.

I added a 2" strip of background fabric to the left side, to give the fish a little water so their noses wouldn't be pressed against the aquarium glass.

Fish on Point

❋ Blocks – Place on point

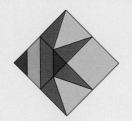

❋ Units

❋ Templates

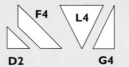

F4 L4 A4
D2 G4

F3 L3 A3
D1 ¹/2 G3

F2 L2 B2
D1 G2

Yardage Schmardage

Assorted Orange Prints:
 ³/4 yard total
Assorted Blue/Water Prints for
 Background and Fillers:
 1 ⁵/8 yards total
First Border: ⁷/8 yard
Second Border: ⁷/8 yard
Third Border: 1 yard

Fabrics

Choose a watery blue fabric for the background. Look for an all-over pattern, since anything directional could be a nightmare to cut and piece. Create the fish with a variety of orange prints. I give totals for cutting, so mix them up. The wonderful border fabric was just sitting on my shelf, waiting for this design. There are some great tropical stripes in many shops, and you may want to find a fabric first then coordinate the Fish blocks and background to it. There are two 8" fish, three 6" fish, and four 4" fish.

❋ Cutting Instructions

Fabric	Templates	Total
Oranges	D2	4
	F4	4
	G4 (left and right)	8
	D1 ¹/2	6
	F3	6
	G3 (left and right)	12
	D1	8
	F2	8
	G2 (left and right)	16
Background	A4	2
	L4	4
	A3	3
	L3	6
	B2	4
	L2	8

Filler Triangles:
 two 4 ¹/2" squares (E4)
 two 8 ¹/4" squares
 six 6 ¹/2" squares

Draw each block the exact size on graph paper, then add a $1/4$" seam allowance to all sides. Use a paper pattern to cut filler triangles. Try to keep the straight of the fabric on the outside of the quilt; you'll find it so much easier to add the border, 4" (finished).

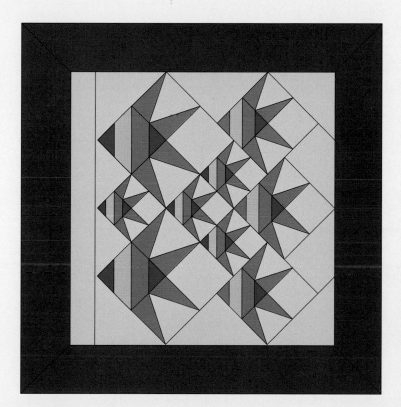

CRUISE FOOD

I've been on so many cruises that some of the absurdities seem normal to me now. I've learned to manage the twelve feedings per day by ordering cold cereal in my room in the morning and passing on the mid-morning snack and afternoon tea. But the event not to be missed is the Grand Buffet, usually served at midnight on the next-to-last night. We quilt-makers can appreciate presentation in any form because of the color and design, and I look forward to the artistic displays on my plate. It just wouldn't be a cruise if the green beans weren't bundled with a strip of red pepper. But on Grand Buffet night they pull out all the stops and do things to food that don't seem legal or moral. One of my all-time favorites in this category was the roasted chicken carcasses (without heads, of course) set up to look like a jazz band, with instruments carved from vegetables. To add to the surrealism, before you can eat any of this decorative food, you are supposed to go through the photo line. No plates, no napkins—just walk past all the food and take pictures. For at least three cruises, I couldn't resist the photo op. I can fill an album with pictures of food. I still go to the Grand Buffet, but I can now leave my camera in the room.

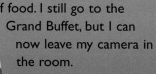

Antigua 38" x 44"

Machine pieced and hand quilted by the author

Antigua

I love this Mutt and Jeff Star block and have used it in quite a few quilts. What I had never done was to put three different scales of blocks in the same quilt. It's relatively easy to mix 12" and 6" blocks. The adventure begins when you add 9" blocks. Nothing lines up directly, so we have to employ a "short seam" approach to assembling the whole quilt (page 34). I used the same idea and technique in designing and constructing Lily and Fish block Cruise Quilts. I love the random look and new dimension the change of scale gives to each piece. The colors are simple. The stars are made from peachy reds, including a plaid with a little turquoise strip. The background and border are different turquoise blues. What makes this quilt special is the Dutch Java bubble-and-wave fabric that I bought in Antigua. At the time I was aggravated that I had to buy a three-yard sarong piece; now I wish they had made me buy six yards because my supply is running low.

Star Blocks

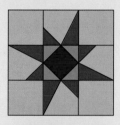

✷ Units

✷ Templates

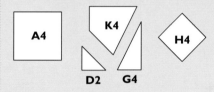

Yardage Schmardage

Background/Water: 1 1/2 yards total

Assorted Peachy Red Prints:
  1 yard total

First Border: 1 1/4 yards

Second Border: 1 1/2 yards

✷ Cutting Instructions

There are three 12" blocks, three 9" blocks and six 6" blocks. Note that one corner in each of the 9" blocks has been altered to accommodate the weird setting. All the others remain whole.

Fabric	Template	Total
Background		
	A4 (shared)	10
	K4	12
	A3	9
	K3	12
	B2	24
	K2	24
Filler strips		

Four 2 1/2" x 6 1/2" strips

One 5 1/2" x 7 1/2" strip

Two 1 1/2" x 9 1/2" strips

One 1 1/2" x 10 1/2" strip

One 3 1/2" x 8 1/2" strip

Three 1 1/2" x 3 1/2" strips

Three 1 1/2" x 2 1/2" strips

One 1 1/2" x 6 1/2" strip

Fabric	Template	Total
Star Points (Peachy Reds)		
	G4	12
	D2	12
	G3	12
	D1 1/2	12

G2	24
D1	24
Center Diamond	
H4	3
H3	3
H2	6
Triangles around Diamonds	
D2	12
D1 ½	12
D1	24

Piece together the units for all blocks. Then make all the 6" blocks. Wait to construct the 12" blocks because of the shared corners. Here's where it starts to get tricky. (Nothing really lines up into tidy rows, so proceed slowly.) To make this go together you need to sew "short seams" to avoid having set in pieces.

Short Seam Technique

Here's the principle that you may have used before in a traditional block, called Bright Hopes.

1. Sew square to first piece, but begin stitching 1" short of the end.

Start here

2. Sew next two strips on as if you were making a Log Cabin block.

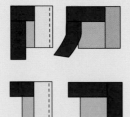

3. Flip loose corner of first strip away from edge and sew on fourth strip.

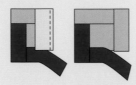

4. Now you can come back to where you originally started the first strip and finish sewing it to the rest of the block. This is harder to explain in words than it is to actually do. But, it's nifty to have in your bag of sewing tricks.

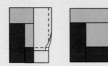

Our goal is never to have to sew into a corner. The method I just described enables us to avoid them. Now for my best advice: Lay the quilt out on a flat vertical surface with all the fill-in pieces in place. Plan only three sewing moves at a time. The worst thing you can do is to get too far ahead of yourself. Look for the seams you can sew from end to end and where you will need to stop short.

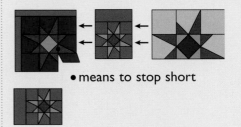

• means to stop short

Add first border 3" (finished) and second border 8" (finished) to complete the quilt.

Nightblooms in Nassau

Nightblooms in Nassau 58" x 58"

Machine pieced by the author and machine quilted by Gayle Wallace

Nightblooms in Nassau

As you can see by the number of lily-quilt variations in this book, I love this design and all the possibilities for expanding and rearranging it. I think its versatility comes from its directional nature. The Lily block has a recognizable top and bottom, left and right, so it can be arranged in countless ways. In this quilt, I added an extra row of units to the basic lily for more petals and greenery. Then I arranged the blocks in a Barn-Raising setting. It could easily be expanded to bed size by adding more blocks to the top, bottom, and sides. I was in the mood for a dark background, so I chose scrap navies and then looked for pinks and a green that would hold up well against the navy. The green is a piece of Dutch Java fabric, which you probably wouldn't recognize if you saw the whole piece. Lots of fussy cutting left me with fabric that looked like mice had been at it, but the effort was worthwhile because the intense yellow-green sparkles off the navy. I think you could have a lot of fun with fabric in this quilt. All the lilies could be different colors. Because the leaves form a secondary pattern of large squares, you can emphasize them by changing the background colors subtly in each square. Get out the colored pencils and play. You could also make copies of the quilt, cut it into the individual blocks, and arrange them in other settings, such as Straight Furrows or Streak of Lightning.

Night Bloom Lily Block

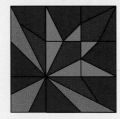

☀ Units

☀ Templates

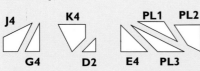

J4   K4   PL1   PL2

G4   D2   E4   PL3

Yardage Schmardage

Assorted Navy Prints for Background, First and Third Borders:
　3 1/2 yards total
Assorted Green Prints:
　1 1/8 yards total
Assorted Pink Prints:
　3 1/4 yards total

☀ Cutting Instructions

Fabric	Template	Total
Background	G4 (left and right)	64
	K4 (left and right)	32
	E4	32
	PL2	32
Green	J4	16
	PL3 (left and right)	32
Pink	J4	32
	G4 (left and right)	64
	D2	32
	PL1	32

Assemble the units. Join the blocks following the illustration. Add the borders, 2" (finished), 1" (finished), and 3" (finished); mitering the corners, to complete the quilt.

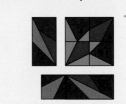

MY DRESSING ROOM SECRET

One of the hardest tasks for any of us with less-than-perfect figures is buying a swimsuit. I suppose I could join a gym and live on celery, and in a year or two actually enjoy the shopping. But I would rather quilt than do stomach curls. And there are too many wonderful things to see in the water to avoid this swimsuit thing completely. But why do they have to put three-way mirrors in the dressing rooms? With practice, you can master my fitting techniques and be ready when the ocean calls. Take as many suits as interest you into the dressing room. Then you don't have to leave that room again until you have made a decision. Now for the hard part: put on the suit but don't look in the mirror. If you have to look, just look at your lovely smile, but at nothing below your neck. Feel around to make sure nothing is hanging out that shouldn't. Bend over to see if the straps will roll off when you are swimming. If it passes all these tests and you like the color, take a deep breath and a quick peek. Then take it off and buy it. Now go look for a wonderful cover-up.

CRUISE
Hawaii

I can remember when Hawaii became a state. I read in my *Weekly Reader*© about the Islands and how they were formed by volcanoes. As the years have gone by, I have had friends who have vacationed there and I've watched television travelogues showing the beauty of the place. I also heard complaints about overbuilding on the beaches and how things had changed, not necessarily for the better. I had even stopped in Honolulu for an hour or two on my way to Australia. But I never imagined going there for a stay. It seemed so far away: I could be in the Caribbean within hours, but would need to fly for a whole day to get to Hawaii.

All this changed when I got a call from Susan Kinkki who lives in Kekaha on the island of Kauai (that all has a wonderful ring to it). She's not fond of flying so, instead of coming to the mainland for quilting events, she arranges to have teachers come to Hawaii to teach. It's all very informal and wonderful fun. The quilters on Kauai are enthusiastic, talented, and great fun to be with. For three years, I stayed with Susan and her family, teaching for two days and lingering for two weeks. And I was enchanted—by the whales, the ocean and beaches, the flora, the chickens, the mountains and canyons, the quilt shop and the quilters. I actually got a little misty when the time came to fly home. I love Kauai so much I just had to take a group from the mainland on tour. Barb Spohn from Specialty Tours was easy to talk into this because she loves the Islands even more than I do, and we added Hawaii to our lists of tours.

Aloha Kauai

Aloha Kauai 37 ³/₄" x 77 ¹/₄"

Machine pieced and hand quilted by the author

Aloha Kauai

With a change of fabric and a little tweaking of the design I transformed an Alaskan quilt into its Hawaiian counterpart. Every winter for the past few years, I've taught on the island of Kauai. The first years there, I gave workshops that I teach everywhere. My good friend Susan Kinkki, who organizes all this, suggested that if I did an Alaskan quilt, it was only right that I design one especially for Hawaii. The first thing I had to deal with was the whale. While we were in Kauai, Susan and her husband Mike took me out in their boat to watch whales. The humpback whales that feed all summer in the waters around Alaska come to Hawaii in the winter to have and make babies. We kept our legal distance from the whales whenever possible, but we couldn't stop one from breaching within thirty yards of the boat. After these close encounters with humpbacks, I found myself dissatisfied with the original pieced whale. So I elongated the grid from the original and added that very distinctive pectoral fin. By shifting their direction and adding triangles to the trees, I created Golden Shower Trees, which are always in bloom when I visit. I borrowed the Long Fish that border the tree section from a Cruise Quilt and drew up my version of the sun to put in the corners. Putting the word "Kauai" in the border was not in the original plan: it was my solution to running out of the perfect border fabric.

The design was good, but I think it's the fabric that makes this quilt. Instead of the cold blues and greens of Alaska, I used the sparkling turquoise of the water and the brilliant pinks, yellows, and oranges of both flowers and fish.

Golden Shower Tree

Make 3 blocks total.

☀ **Templates**

B2 D2 E3 TT D1 Optional

Yardage Schmardage

For Center Panel:

Background (Solid blue or tone-on-tone): 1/2 yard total

Setting Triangles (Water print): 1 yard total

Yellow/Gold Print: 1/8 yard total

Brown: 1/8 yard total (or scraps)

Red/Orange Floral Border: 1/4 yard total

Yellow/Orange Corner Fish: 1/8 yard total

For Little Fish Border:

Background (Blue, including spacers and next border): 5/8 yard total

Assorted Bright Prints: 1/2 yard total

For Whales:

Background (Water print): 1 yard total

Black Prints: 5/8 yard total

Black/White Prints: 1/4 yard total

Filler Rectangles (Light Tropical Print): 3/8 yard total

For Sun Corners:

Background (Blue): 1/4 yard total, plus scraps from whales and filler rectangles.

Assorted Orange/Yellow Prints: 1/8 yard total

For Outside Border (unpieced and mitered corners): 2 5/8 yards

☼ Cutting Instructions

Fabric	Template	Total
Background (Blue)		
	B2	12
	D2	51
	D1 (optional)	10
	E3	6
Yellow/Gold	D2	51
	D1 (optional)	30
Brown	TT	3

You can cut these triangles out using templates. Even quicker is 2" triangle paper (see Sources, page 78). Follow the instructions on the paper, and you'll find this method works like a dream.

Very Little Fish

Make 12

I used very Little Fish (2" finished) for the cornerstones of the floral border around the shorter trees.

☼ Templates

D2   D1

☼ Cutting Instructions

Fabric	Template	Total
Background	D1	36
Floral for fish body		
	D2	12
Floral for fish tail		
	D1	12

Center Panel Construction

For the borders of the Tree blocks, cut twelve 2 1/2" x 10 1/2" strips. I used a floral fabric to remind myself of leis. Sew a very Little Fish block to both ends of the top and bottom border pieces, then sew the borders to each Tree block (with the very Little Fish blocks at each corner).

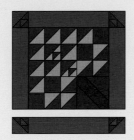

14"
Finished

For the Center Panel Triangles, cut twelve 14" quarter-square triangles from scenic aquatic-themed fabric. Although these filler triangles are quarter-square triangles, you must cut them as if they are half-square triangles so the straight grain runs the length and width of the quilt. In other words, you don't want to sew the next borders to a bias, stretchy edge.

If you make a paper pattern for the triangles, first draw a 14" line. From the middle of this line, mea-

sure 7". Connect this point to the ends. Add 1/4" seam allowance all the way around. Then, cut triangles with straight grains on the two short sides.

To complete the Center Panel, sew the triangles to the Tree blocks. Make three blocks total; then sew these units together.

Little Long Fish

Make 28

☼ Templates

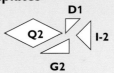

D1
Q2   I-2
G2

☼ Cutting Instructions

Fabric	Template	Total
Background	G2	112
	D1	56
Fish	Q2	28
	I-2	28

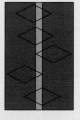

I wanted to do something clever with my Long Fish blocks, which would allow me to use more fabric. So I sewed strips of fabric together to equal an 8" piece. I made this strip wide so I could move the template from side to side and catch different sections of the strips with each fish. I don't know if this was necessary, but it was fun. You can probably cut tail pieces (I-2) from the leftover pieces.

Sew the background Gs to the fish body. Sew the tail pieces together and attach to the fish body. As you can see from the quilt diagram, I planned spacers between all the fish. These pieces are background fabric cut 1 1/2" x 2 1/2". Now look carefully at the photograph of the quilt. I can't explain it but some of my fish are sewn nose to tail with no spaces between. And the quilt is flat so it must have been necessary. I then added another 1 1/2" border (1" finished) around all the fish.

Humpback Whales

Use the instructions of the Humpback Whales on page 50 as a guide.

✹ Units

Make 4 (Right)

Make 4 (Left)

Cut spacer strips 5 1/2" x 7 1/2" and 3 1/2" x 7 1/2". Then, sew rows of Whales together with spacers between them. You can trim the end spacers to fit the quilt as needed.

Last but not least...

Corner Squares with Sun Sections

You will have to make a decision on how you would like to piece this: appliqué is even an option and the only one I didn't try. But I did sew each corner differently in my search for the perfect method.

Method 1: Make exact size templates from page 63. Trace around templates on wrong side of fabric and cut, adding 1/4" seam allowance. Hand piece with short running stitch. Pin pieces together by matching pencil lines.

Method 2: Same as Method 1, only machine stitch on pencil line instead of hand stitching.

Method 3: Trace templates four times, page 63, on freezer–paper.

Cut apart and iron on the back side of the fabric. Using a rotary cutter and small Omnigrid® ruler, cut pieces out, adding 1/4" all the way around. You'll probably need to cut curved edges with scissors, eyeballing 1/4" seam. Pin pieces together, matching edges of freezer paper. Machine stitch along edges of paper. Assemble "pointy ring" first, then sew to quarter-circle and lastly sew to L-shaped piece.

Method 4: Paper-piecing, or the "Sew-and-Flip" technique. You'll need a working knowledge of this type of piecing before trying this method. Copy the pattern on page 62 four times. Cut apart the pieces into three sections: a quarter-circle, pointy arc, and L-shaped piece. Paper-piece background and "sun" fabrics into an arc. Add quarter-circle and L shape by sewing machine. Mark seam lines with pencil and match to seam line of arcs.

Method 5: Choose something else for these corner squares. Finished size needs to be 7". You could use a big tropical floral print as is, or appliqué something appropriate (hibiscus, or sea turtles, or rainbows).

Sew corner squares to whales for top and bottom rows.

Add final borders, 7" (finished). As I said, "The only reason I pieced 'Kauai' into my border is because I ran out of border fabric. It was just too perfect not to use."

You can arrange all these elements in innumerable ways. You could even make my quilt design bed-size by doing two rows of trees. Make more Little Long Fish and Whales to fill the space.

I may be sounding like a broken record, but I really hope you will use my ideas and quilts as a jumping-off point. Change things, add things, and make the quilt really your own.

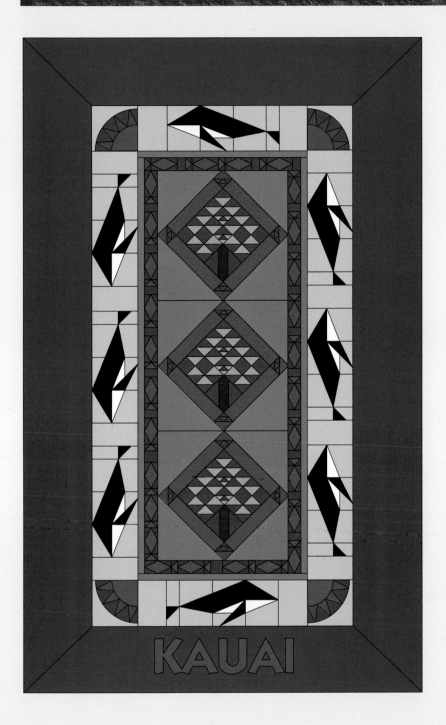

KAUAI

PAPARAZZA

Most of my life I've been "a day late and a dollar short." Trust me to pick the grocery line with a price check or to leave a slot machine just before it pays off. But just once I did the right thing at the right time. I was in Kauai. My friend Susan and I were heading to the little protected beach near Spouting Horn that we call "the aquarium," to go snorkeling. I'd been having trouble with my ears, so we stopped to pick up earplugs. I bought the earplugs and then I noticed disposable underwater cameras. Should I buy one or just save the money? For once, I did the right thing and bought the camera. When we arrived at the beach, a big monk seal (endangered and unique to the Hawaiian Islands) was snoozing and digesting his dinner—my first photo opportunity. Then I got in the water and found myself hovering over a fish-cleaning station. Two yellow-and-purple wrasses were working as fast as they could to clean parasites from at least a dozen fish lined up (as well as fish line up) waiting for the service. I'd heard of this but had never actually seen it—photo op #2. I swam out a little farther and was looking around when a huge sea turtle (also endangered) swam right under me. It's hard to shout for joy while breathing through a snorkel, but I did manage to take a few pictures before it swam out of sight.

Hawaiian Spinning Stars 44" x 56"
Machine pieced and hand quilted by the author

Hawaiian Spinning Stars

I've been teaching on Kauai, the garden island of Hawaii, for a few years and have enjoyed shopping at one of the best quilt shops–not only on the islands but anywhere. Kapaia Stitchery in Lihue carries beautiful tropicals seldom seen on the mainland as well as many of the best quilt fabrics available. One of my favorite discoveries was a fabulous poppy fabric–large flowers (8" across) in yellows, oranges, and reds on a turquoise background. I chose other fabrics that captured the exuberance of the original print. I wasn't sure just where the poppy print would go, but knew it would make the quilt. You are probably looking at the quilt, wondering what I am talking about. Try as I might, the only good place I found to put the poppies was on the back! The colors were good; reminding me of the sun, sea, and flowers; and the design was interesting, so I carried on despite my temporary disappointment. I love what this easy-to-piece block does when several are set next to each other. It is a simple Nine-Patch composed of Ice Cream Cones and Ribbons but it gives an impression of the Mutt and Jeff star in an off-kilter setting. I extended the points into a wide swath of background. I made it wall-hanging size because of fabric limitations. It would be easy to enlarge this quilt to fit any bed, and to tone it down so you could stand to go into the room.

Spinning Star Block

Make 6 blocks total.

✺ Units

✺ Templates

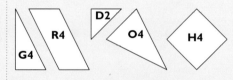

Yardage Schmardage

Background (Turquoise):
  1 1/2 yard total
Yellow: 1 1/3 yard total
  (includes second Border)
If you want to use a different yellow fabric for the stars, an additional 1/4 yard total will be needed.
Orange print: 1/8 yard total
Red print: 1 5/8 yard total
  (includes third Border)
Multi-Print: 3/4 yard total

✺ Cutting Instructions

Fabric	Template	Total
Turquoise	O4	24
	G4(left only)	48
Yellow Print	G4(right only)	24
	D2	24
Orange print	D2	24
Red print	H4	6
Multi-print	R4(left only)	24
	G4(left only)	34
(includes 10 for first border)		

✺ Construction Instructions

For the blocks: Piece units as illustrated. Combine units into three rows, and then sew rows together. Make 6 total.

For the first border: Cut seven 4 1/2" strips of turquoise; then cut four of the strips into 12 1/2" sections. You should be able to get three from one 4 1/2" strip.

Using the diagram as a guide, use the G4 template to cut the left end at an angle.

Cut

Sew a G4 piece of the multi-print to the cut end. Make 6 total.

For the corner pieces, cut the fifth strip of turquoise into 8 1/2" sections and repeat the process above to add G4 pieces of the multi-print. Make 4 total.

For the remaining corner pieces, cut the last strip of turquoise into 12 1/2" sections (no piecing).

Sew the blocks together and add the first border, following the diagram. I mitered the corners, but it's not necessary.

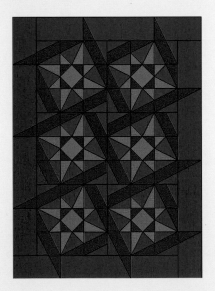

Add second border 1" (finished), and third border, 5" (finished).

CRUISE Alaska

We took our first cruise through the Inside Passage from Vancouver to Anchorage in 1993. I don't know what I expected, but I certainly didn't anticipate the mind-boggling beauty of the place. I'd seen Alaskan calendar pictures and nature programs on TV, but neither prepared me for the hugeness, the rawness, and the serenity of the scenery.

I designed these quilts with elements that symbolize Alaska—whales, pine trees, stars, mountains. All of the quilts have some of these elements, so I will give general directions for their construction. When you can piece both Whales, a Pine Tree, the Sitka Spruce, and the small off-kilter Star blocks, you can make any of the Alaskan quilts.

Alaska Quilt Blocks

You can design your own versions of these quilts, and I encourage you to do so. Feel free to add elements I haven't even thought of. One of my students bordered her quilt with Delectable Mountains, and another pieced Lighthouses for her border.

Star Block

6" square (finished).

✵ Units

If you are making several Stars, consider the reverse Star as well. Then you can cut the unit Ks and the Gs on doubled fabric. (It took me three quilts to figure that one out.)

✵ Templates

✵ Cutting Instructions per block

Fabric	Template	Total
Blue	B2	4
	K2 (left or right)	4
White or Silvery Gray		
	B2	1
	D1	4
	G2 (left or right)	4

Sitka Spruce Block

4" x 10" (finished)

✵ Units

✵ Templates

✵ Cutting Instructions per block

Fabric	Template	Total
Green	L4	1
	I-4	2
Lt. Blue	G4 (left and right)	2
	D2	4

To make trunk section, cut two 2 1/4" strips of background fabric. Cut one 1" strip brown fabric for the trunk. Then, sew background fabric to sides of trunk strip. Press seams toward trunk.

To vary the heights of the trees, cut shorter trunk sections, and compensate at top with strip of background fabric. You won't have to match all those points if you use this method.

Pine Tree Block

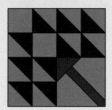

8" square
(finished).

☀ Units

☀ Templates

| B2 | D2 / D2 | N4 |

There are ten green/blue triangle squares per pine tree. If you are only making a few trees you could cut the shapes with templates. For lots of trees, consider using triangle paper 2" (finished). Vary the dark green fabrics to make it more interesting.

☀ Cutting Instructions per block

Fabric	Template	Total
Background	B2	2
	D2	6
	N4	1
Brown	D2	1
Green	D2	6

Cut a 1" strip of brown for trunk. Sew triangle units, using the illustrations as a guide.

Make trunk unit by splitting N4 from corner to middle of blunt side.

Cut

Sew 1" strip to cut side. Leave extra at the corner end.

Sew other side on and trim off excess trunk. Press toward trunk.

Sew triangle (brown) to blunt end.

Arrange the four units and sew together, using the illustration as a guide.

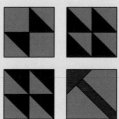

Bear Paw with Salmon

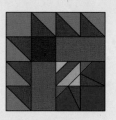

8" square
(finished).

☀ Units

☀ Templates

| B2 | C4 |
| K2 / F2 / D2 |
| D1 G2 |

☀ Cutting Instructions per block

Fabric	Template	Total
Background Blue #1		
	B2	1
	D2	6
Background Blue #2		
	B2	1
	K2	2
Brown #1	B2	1
Brown #2	D2	6
	G2	2
Brown #3	C4	2
Pink/Peachy Reds		
	D1	4
	F2	2

Arrange the four units and sew together, using the illustration as a guide.

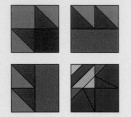

Whale Block

6" x 14" (finished).

☀ Units

This was my first whale, and it looked pretty whale-like to me. Because there are several one-way only pieces, it is easier to make two whales than one. One will swim left; the other one will swim right. I've designed all the quilts to use equal numbers of left and right whales.

☀ Templates

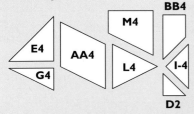

☀ Cutting Instructions per block

Fabric	Template	Total
Background	E4	1
	G4	3
	M4	1
	BB4	1
	D2	1
Black print	E4	1
	AA4	1
	L4	1
	I-4	1
Black/white print		
	G4	2

Sew together in vertical units. Then sew vertical rows together.

The largest of these whales is based on a 4" unit and templates. To make the smaller whale, use a 3" unit and templates. The littlest whale is based on a 2" unit and templates.

☀ Smaller Whale

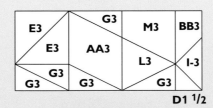

4 1/2" x 10 1/2" (finished).

☀ Littlest Whale

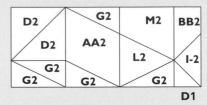

3" x 7" (finished).

☀ The Humpback Whale Block

7" x 17" (finished).

☀ Units

The Humpback Whale was designed originally for the Kauai quilt. Every winter I teach on Kauai (an excellent place to work when one lives in Wisconsin). My friend Susan Kinkki challenged me to make a Hawaiian quilt since I had done the Alaskan quilts. Her husband Mike takes us out in his boat every year to watch the humpbacks, which Susan insists "come to party in Kauai." Having seen these leviathans of the sea up-close and personal, I wasn't happy with the original whale. It was too squatty. So I elongated the grid and added the pectoral fin. The sheer numbers of odd-shaped templates may appear daunting, but the block is big and goes together more easily than you might imagine. I've taught this in one-day workshops and many students have a few whales done before lunch. One student even used the small drawing to paper piece a truly mini whale. I won't go there.

❋ Templates

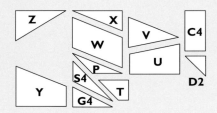

Because of the many one-way-only templates, cut fabric doubled, which doubles the numbers of each template and makes two whales, one swimming left, one swimming right.

❋ Cutting Instructions per block

The most confusing phase of making the humpback whale can be the cutting. If you follow these steps, it should be easy:

1. Layout all the pieces following the illustration. A few templates do double duty as head and background or background "underbelly" and "under tail."

2. Isolate the whale body templates. Trace around templates on doubled fabric and cut out with scissors or rotary cutter and ruler. You can

squeeze the templates closer together so you won't waste fabric.

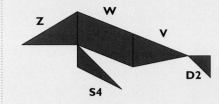

3. Layout cut fabric pieces in the same order as templates. If you just pile up the fabric, you can get in all kinds of trouble.

4. Pick out the underbelly templates X and P and cut one of each per whale.

5. Layout background templates in order around cut whale pieces, using the illustration as a guide.

This is especially helpful if you are using a wavy water print. The Y and T templates are the only templates you will need two of per whale. Again close up the spaces to use less fabric. Trace around the templates and cut with scissors or rotary cutter. As you cut, place the background pieces in order around the whale pieces.

Now you can start sewing. Work in vertical rows.

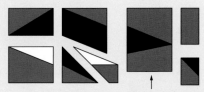

Press toward background

Put rows together.

Ketchikan 64" x 93"

Machine pieced and hand quilted by the author

Ketchikan

This is the first of the Alaskan quilts. I had toyed with the idea of working with totem-pole imagery, but I found I just didn't know enough about them to do the subject justice. I think the idea had an influence on the shape of this quilt though. The breakthrough was when I came up with the first whale design, though my Alaskan friends say it more closely resembles a halibut. The center block is a little obscure. I added two toes to the Bear Paw design, then put what I had hoped looked like a salmon in the bear's paw. Well, maybe not, but it seemed like a good idea at the time.

Yardage Schmardage

Background, Assorted Blue Prints (water, sky, snow–for trees, mountains, bear paws, stars and pieced whales/second border):

  3 1/4 yards total (can use leftover fabric from Borders Three and Four)

Medium-dark Blue tone-on-tone–Border Three:

  2 5/8 yards total

Dark Blue Print–Border Four:

  2 7/8 yards total

Assorted Green tone-on-tone or small prints (includes First Border and Sashing): 1 1/2 yards total

Brown: 5/8 yard total

Assorted Pink/Peach tone-on-tone or small prints: 1/4 yard total

White or Silvery Gray (for Stars):

  1/4 yard total

Assorted Black Prints

  (for whale bodies): 7/8 yard total

Assorted White and Black Prints

  (for whale bellies): 1/8 yard total

Pine Tree Block

Make eight Pine Tree blocks, following the instructions on page 49.

Sitka Spruce Block

Make eight Sitka Spruce blocks using mountain-color fabrics and four Sitka Spruce blocks using tree-color fabrics; following the instructions on page 48.

Bear Paw Blocks with Salmon

Make four Bear Paws with Salmon, following the illustrations on page 49.

☀ **Units**

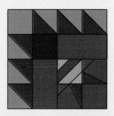

Center Cross Block

Make one Center Cross Block (A4) with crossed trunks, using the drawing as a guide.

And use template A4 to cut two from a theme fabric.

Star Blocks

Make ten 6" Star blocks, following the instructions on page 48.

Make 10 (Right).

❋ Large Whale Blocks

Make six Large Whale blocks 6" x 14" (finished), following the instructions on page 50.

Make 3 (Right).

Make 3 (Left).

❋ Small Whale blocks

Make four Small Whale blocks 4 1/2" x 10 1/2" (finished), following the instructions on page 50.

Make 2 (Right).

Make 2 (Left).

For the Center Panel, make the Small Whales fit with the Stars and Large Whales by sewing a 2" strip to top or bottom of the blocks.

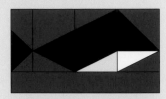

Sew the blocks together, then join the units, using the illustration as a guide. Set blocks together with 1 1/2" strips of green.

Using the illustration as a guide, sew the whales and stars together to the center panel for left and right sides. Note the blank rectangle at the top of the left row and bottom of the right row. This is your adjuster: Use these rectangular strips to adjust the measurement of the blocks, as needed.

Cut two 6 1/2" squares (the adjusters) and sew one to the last star on each border strip. Trim off excess after you have sewn rows to center section. Add last border, 5" (finished), to complete the quilt, mitering the corners.

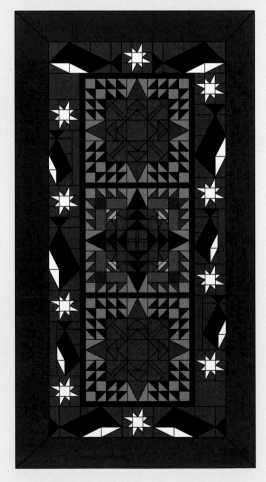

Skagway

Skagway 46" x 72" (Top only)
Machine pieced by the author

Skagway

Our third stop on the cruise up the Inside Passage is the small town of Skagway, nestled on the water and surrounded by mountains. I had gone a little overboard on the size and complexity of *Juneau* and decided that for this quilt maybe "less is more." The center of the quilt is composed of four Pine Trees with trunks to the middle. I had designed the Humpback Whales for my trip to Hawaii and knew they had to go into this quilt. The little off-kilter Stars fill the corners, with the addition of a one-inch strip of background to bring them up to the needed size. I added a row of Sitka Spruce to the top and bottom to creat a rectangular quilt.

Yardage Schmardage

Assorted Blue Prints
(Background for trees and whales):
  2 1/8 yards total
Blue Snowflake Print
(Setting Strips and Outer Border):
  2 1/2 yards total
Rust
(Tree Trunks and Inner Borders):
  1 3/8 yards total
Assorted Green Tone-on-Tone or
Small Prints (for trees):
  5/8 yard total
Assorted Black Prints
(for whale bodies):
  1/2 yard total
White and Gray Print
(for whale bellies):
  1/4 yard total
White or Silvery Gray Print
(for stars) :
  1/4 yards total

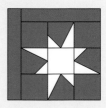

Pine Tree Blocks

Make four Pine Trees blocks 8" (finished), following the instructions on page 49. Sew blocks together, with trunks meeting at the center.

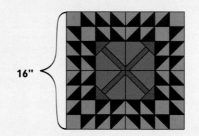

16"

Sew 2" border around the Pine Tree center panel. (I made a border strip (1/2" finished) of rust fabric, (1" finished) blue fabric, and again (1/2" finished) rust fabric strips, and mitered the corners.)

Humpback Whales

Make four Humpback Whale blocks 7" x 17" (finished), with two swimming right and two swimming left.

Right

Left

I made the whales the same length as the center section by adding a 1 1/2" strip (1" finished) to nose end and a 2 1/2" strip (2" finished) to tail end.

Star Blocks

Make four Star blocks 6" (finished). Sew 1 1/2" (1" finished) strips to adjacent sides, using the illustration as a guide.

Sew stars to each end of top and bottom whale blocks, with spacing strips toward outside corners, using the illustration as a guide.

Sew whales to each side of center panel section.

Sew 1 1/2" border (1" finished) of rust fabric to the center panel. Then add a 2 1/2" strip of outer border fabric to top and bottom of the panel.

Sitka Spruce Block

Make 16 Sitka Spruce blocks 4" x 10" (finished), following the instructions on page 48.

Cut 2 1/2" and 1 1/2" trunk sections, varying trunk lengths, as needed. Compensate for shorter trunks by adding background strips to tops of shorter trees.

Sew two rows each of eight Trees. Add 1 1/2" (1" finished) strips to either end of Tree rows, using the illustration as a guide. Then sew Sitka Spruce rows to top and bottom of center section, using the illustration as a guide.

Add border, 6" (finished) to complete the quilt. (This is where I used the great snowflake print fabric.)

Juneau 70" x 106" (Top only)
Machine pieced by the author

Juneau

The next Alaskan quilt started with the medallion idea. I wanted a bed-sized rectangular quilt, so I started with three Pine Trees on point in the center. As you can see, I added Little Stars to the fill-in triangles. Feel free to leave these out: they were a lot of trouble for slight effect. The next row is smaller whales 4 1/2" x 10 1/2" (finished) with Stars in the corners. Sitka Spruces make up the next row. Note how I brought the trees down each side in single file. If you want the quilt to get wider at this point, consider having the trees point outward all around the quilt. (If you choose to do this, you will have to recalculate for the next row of whales and probably fiddle with the spacers between the whales.) I looked for fabrics in shades of blue that felt cold, and I found some wonderful snowflake fabrics. I even found a piece that pictured all the North American animals—caribou, grizzly bear, Arctic hare, ptarmigan, polar bear, seal, and eagle. Whatever possessed the designer to add penguins to the menagerie? Did he or she actually think there were penguins in the northern hemisphere? I cut carefully to avoid getting so much as a penguin's beak in the quilt. The key fabric, but the one used the least, is the rust. It adds just the right amount of warmth and keeps this quilt from being deadly cold.

Yardage Schmardage

Assorted Blue Prints—
Background for trees, stars and whales 4 1/8 yards total (can use leftover fabric from borders Five and Six)

Medium Blue Print—Border Five (unpieced and cut length of fabric) 3 yards total

Dark Blue Print—Border Six (unpieced and cut length of fabric) 3 1/2 yards total

Assorted Green tone-on-tone or small prints (for trees) 3/4 yard total

Rust (tree trunks and Borders One, Two, Three and Four) 3 yards total

White or Silvery Gray (for stars) 3/8 yards total

Assorted Black Prints (for whale bodies) 1 1/4 yard total

Assorted White and Black Prints (for whale bellies) 1/4 yard total

CENTER PANEL Pine Tree Blocks

Make three Pine Tree blocks using 2" triangle paper, following the instructions on page 49.

Star Blocks

Make four Eight-Point Star blocks 4" (finished), using the illustration as a guide.

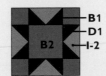

Make four Four-Point Star blocks 3" (finished), using the illustration as a guide.

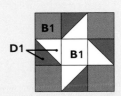

Side Triangles

Cut two E4 and one I-4 for each star. Then make four triangles, which will be slightly larger than what you need. You can use an 8" half-square triangle template to trim the two short sides. Although you will lose a little off the corners of the stars, it will fit perfectly.

8" half-square triangle

Corner Triangles

Sew two E3 units to the small star, using the illustration as a guide. Note that the triangle units will also be too large for the block sides. Just use an 8" quarter-square triangle template to trim off the long side, as needed.

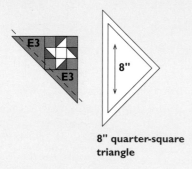

8" quarter-square triangle

Sew the blocks together to complete the center panel. Add a 1 1/2" (1" finished) border of the rust fabric to the center panel, mitering the corners.

CENTER PIECED BORDER
Small Whale Blocks

Sew eight Small Whale blocks 4 1/2" x 10 1/2" (finished), following the instructions on page 50.

Make 4 (Right)

Make 4 (Left)

Sew 2" strip (1 1/2" finished) of the background fabric to the top half of

four of the whale blocks for one side border and to the bottom of the other four whale blocks for the opposite border. Refer to the illustration on page 54 as a guide.

Small Star Blocks

Make 4 Small Star blocks 6" (finished).

Cut and sew 3 1/2" strips of background fabric to the end of each row of whales. Align the center pieced borders with the center panel and trim off excess background fabric, as needed.

Sew whales to each side of center panel. Then sew stars to both ends of the top and bottom whale. Sew the border section to the quilt.

Add 1 1/2" strips (1" finished) of the rust fabric to the center section to border the quilt so far.

Sitka Spruce Border

Make 28 Sitka Spruce blocks 4" x 10" (finished), following the instructions on page 48.

Vary the tree height by cutting shorter trunks and compensating with various widths of background fabric at the top.

Sew nine tree blocks together for top and bottom rows. Sew five trees into a long thin row for left side of

quilt; repeat for right side.

Add tree rows to the quilt, using the illustration as a guide. Border with 1 1/2" strips (1" finished) of the rust fabric, mitering the corners.

Large Whale Border

Make 14 Large Whale Blocks 6" x 14" (finished), following the instructions on page 50.

Make 7 (Right)

Make 7 (Left)

Sew 1 1/2" strips (1" finished) of the background fabric to the top half seven of the whales for one side border and to the bottom of the other seven whales for the opposite border, using the illustration on page 54 as a guide.

Cut 4 1/2" strips of background fabric to use as whale adjuster blocks (refer to quilt diagram on page 61 for placement). Trim excess fabric, as needed. This gives what I call "gimme" space. Work with your quilt and don't be a slave to the numbers.

Add final borders, rust 1", and blue 06" total, (finished), to complete the quilt, following the illustration as a guide. The quilt is big so don't skimp on size with the last border.

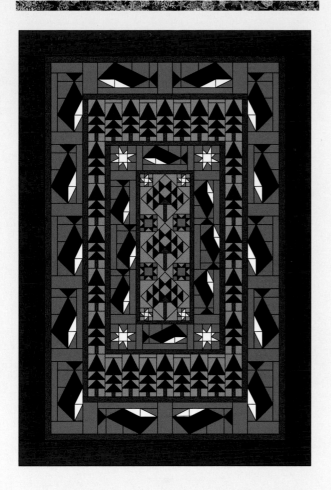

Yardage Chart

The numbers of units you can cut are approximate, depending upon fabric width and template layout.

Units	Size	1/4 yd	1/2 yd.	3/4 yd.	1 yd.
	4 x 4	16	32	48	64
	3 x 3	24	60	84	120
	2 x 2	48	112	160	224
	4 x 2	24	56	80	112
	3 x 1 1/2	40	80	130	170
	4 x 4	16	48	80	112
	3 x 3	40	80	120	180
	2 x 2	84	168	252	336
	1 1/2 x 1 1/2	96	224	352	480
	4"	42	84	140	182
	3"	64	128	192	256
	4 x 4	14	42	70	98
	3 x 3	30	80	130	180
	4 x 4	16	32	56	80
	3 x 3	20	60	90	120
	4 x 4	14	42	70	98
	3 x 3	36	72	108	162
	2 x 2	78	156	236	312
	4 x 2	40	88	128	176
	3 x 1 1/2	60	120	180	260
	2 x 1	128	256	384	528
	4"	16	48	80	112
	3"	40	80	120	180
	4"	20	40	60	80
	3"	28	70	112	158
	4"	20	48	80	110
	3"	40	88	142	196
	4 x 4	12	36	60	84
	3 x 3	28	56	98	126
	4"	32	80	128	192
	3"	60	120	200	280
	4 x 4	20	40	60	80
	3 x 3	28	70	98	140

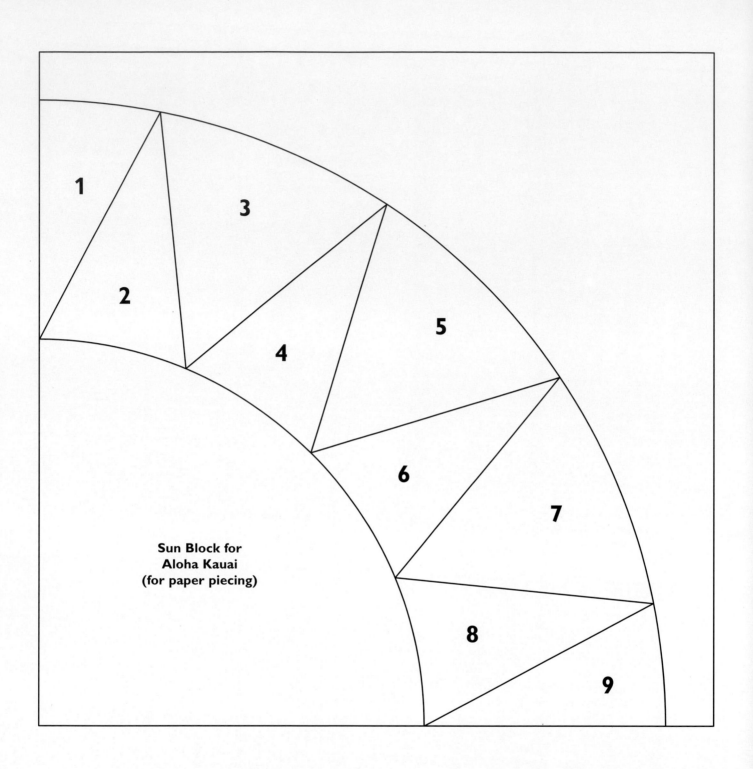

**Sun Block for
Aloha Kauai
(for paper piecing)**

1
2
3
4
5
6
7
8
9

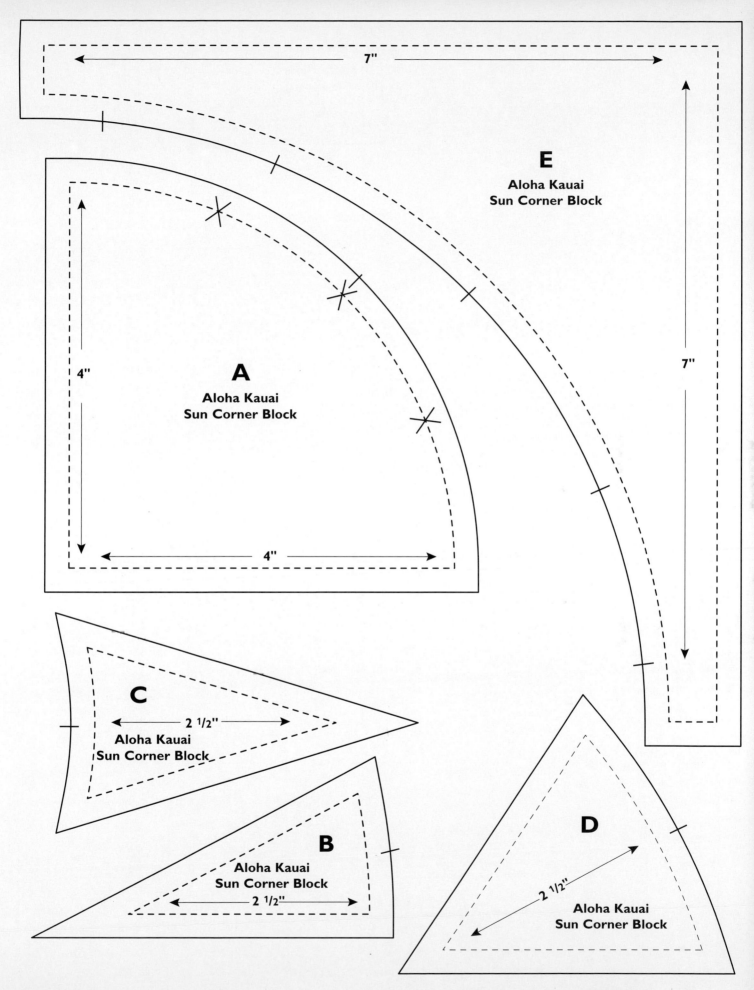

7"

E
Aloha Kauai
Sun Corner Block

4"

A
Aloha Kauai
Sun Corner Block

4"

7"

C
2 1/2"
Aloha Kauai
Sun Corner Block

B
Aloha Kauai
Sun Corner Block
2 1/2"

D
2 1/2"
Aloha Kauai
Sun Corner Block

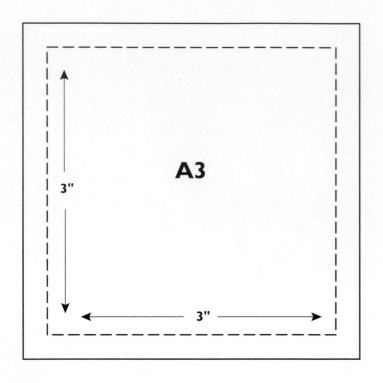

A3

3"

3"

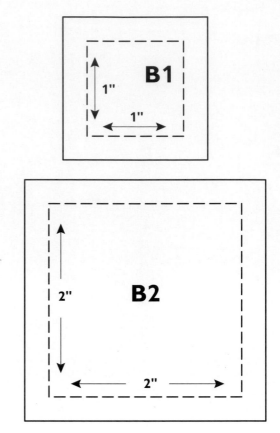

B1

1"

1"

B2

2"

2"

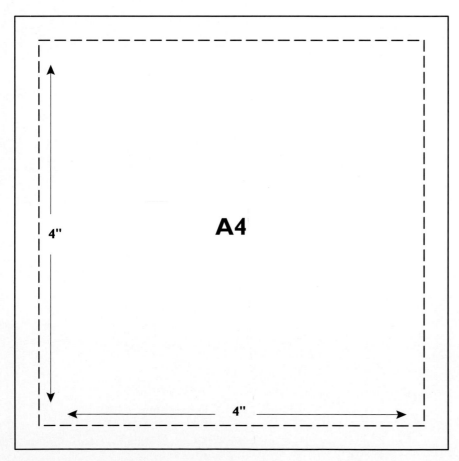

A4

4"

4"

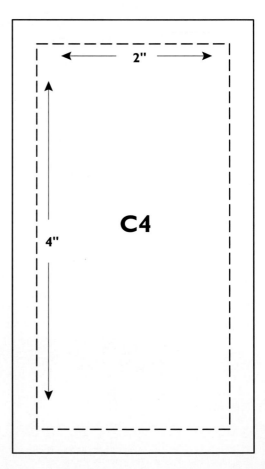

C4

2"

4"

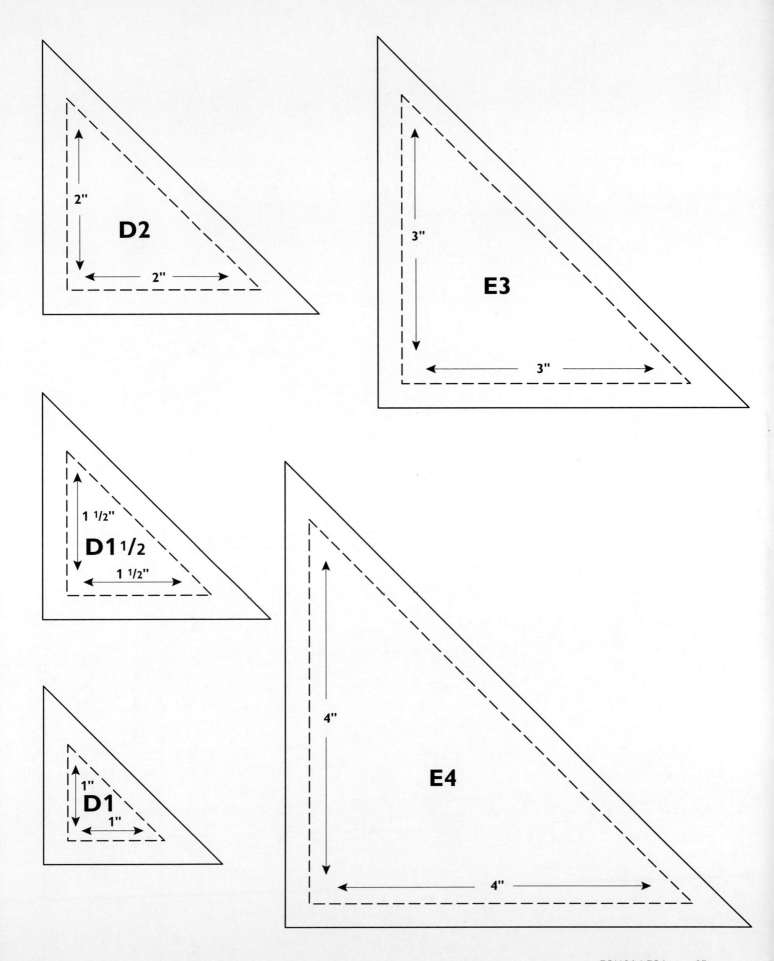

D2

2"

2"

D1 1/2

1 1/2"

1 1/2"

D1

1"

1"

E3

3"

3"

E4

4"

4"

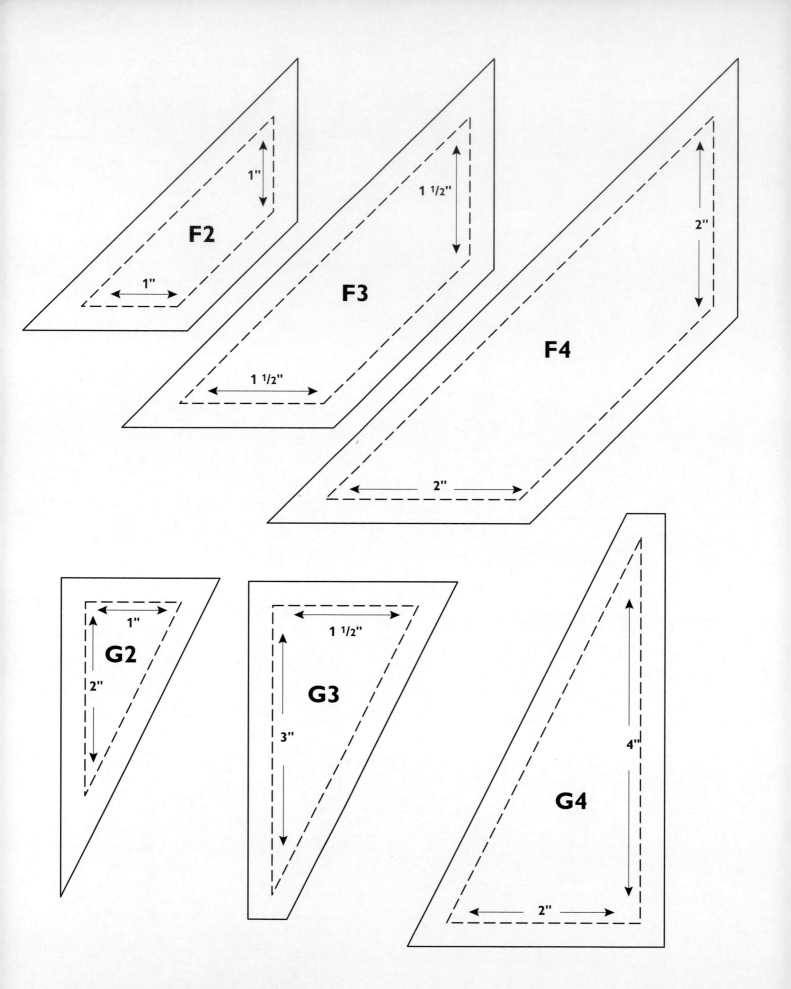

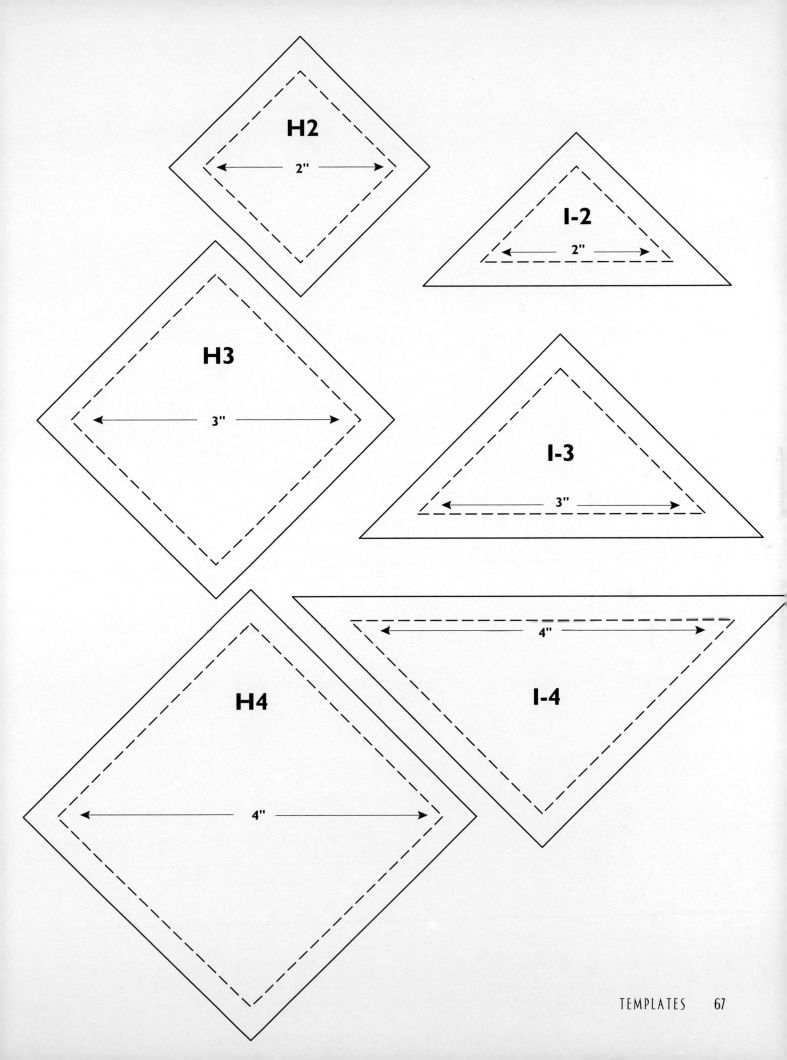

H2

2"

I-2

2"

H3

3"

I-3

3"

H4

4"

I-4

4"

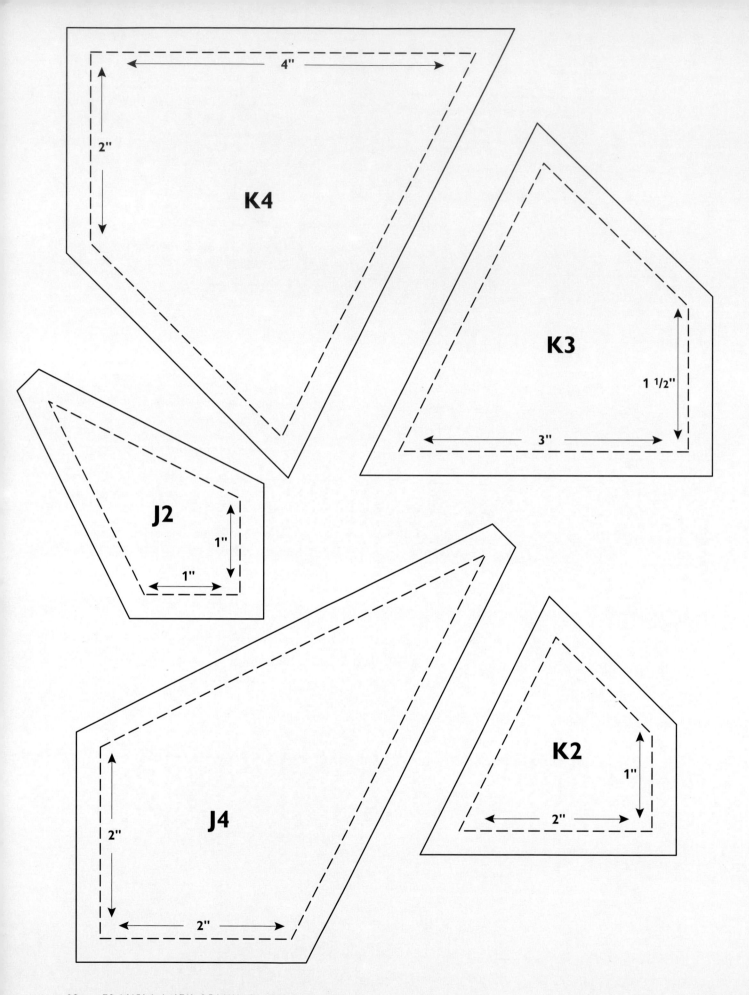

K4

2"

4"

K3

1 1/2"

3"

J2

1"

1"

J4

2"

2"

K2

1"

2"

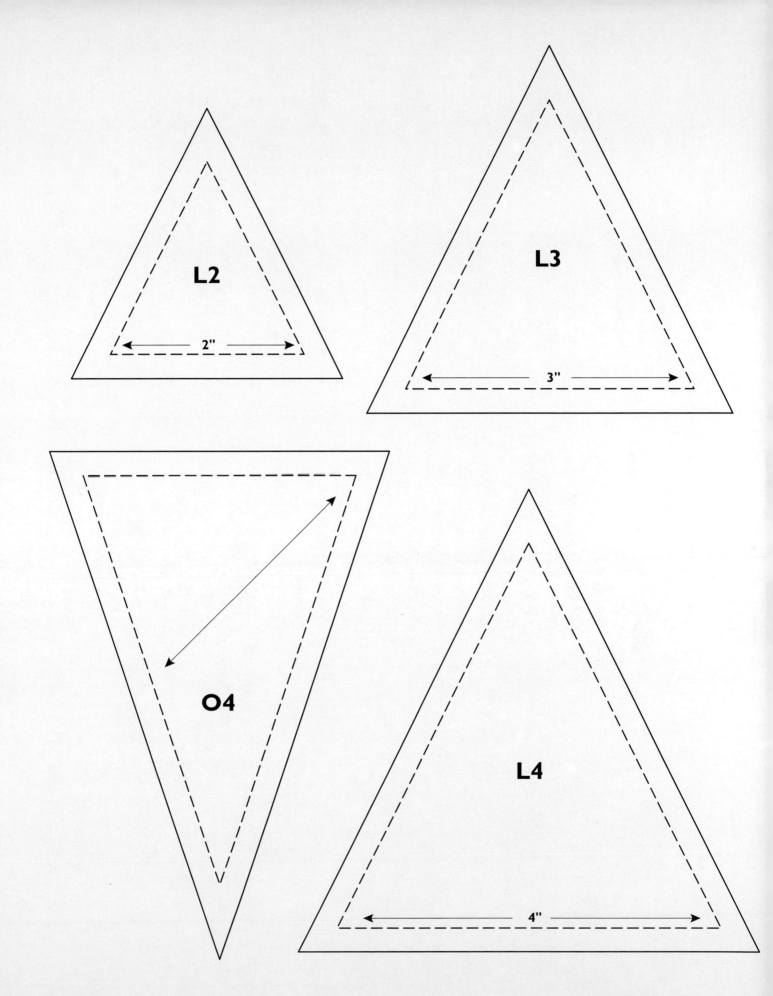

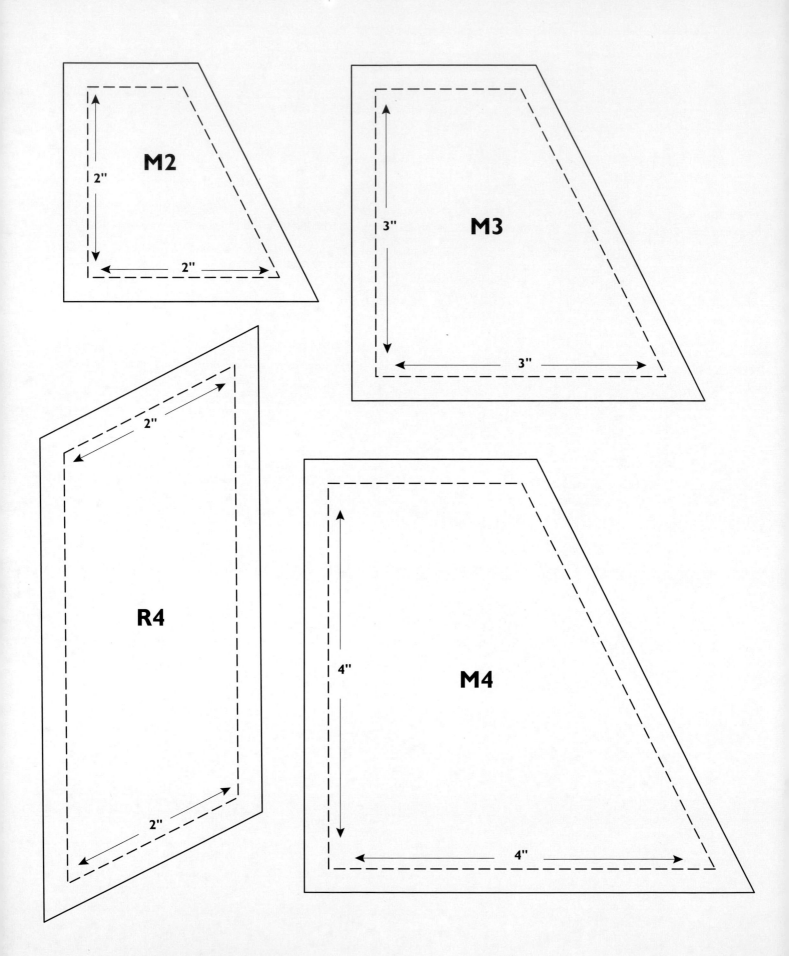

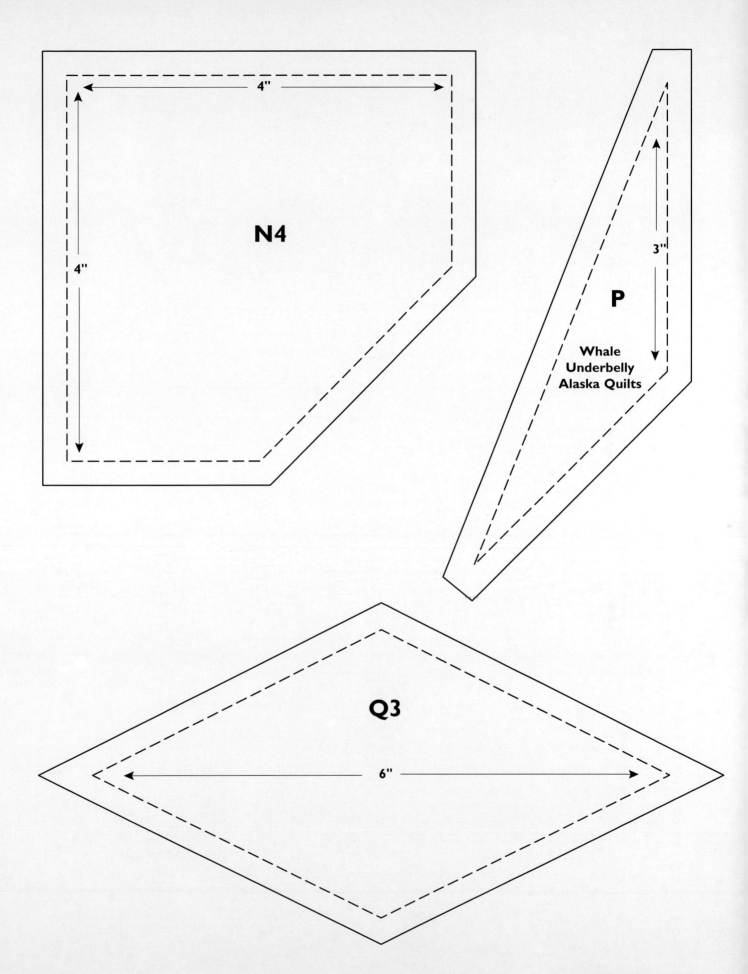

N4

4"

4"

P

3"

Whale Underbelly Alaska Quilts

Q3

6"

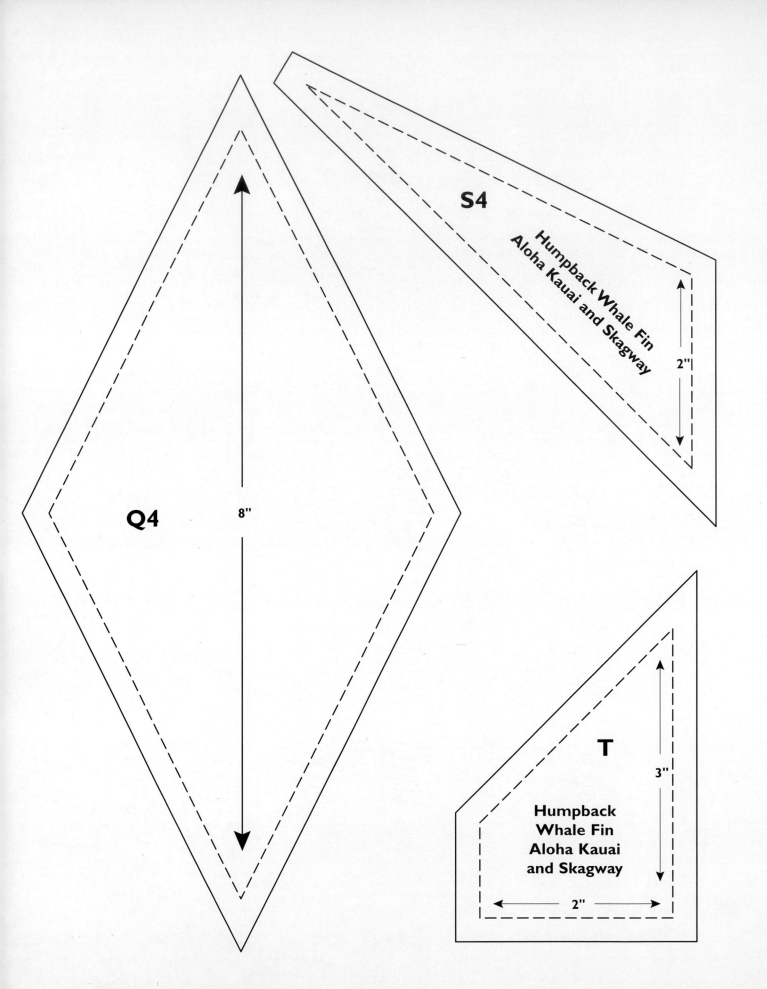

Q4

8"

S4

Humpback Whale Fin
Aloha Kauai and Skagway

2"

T

3"

Humpback
Whale Fin
Aloha Kauai
and Skagway

2"

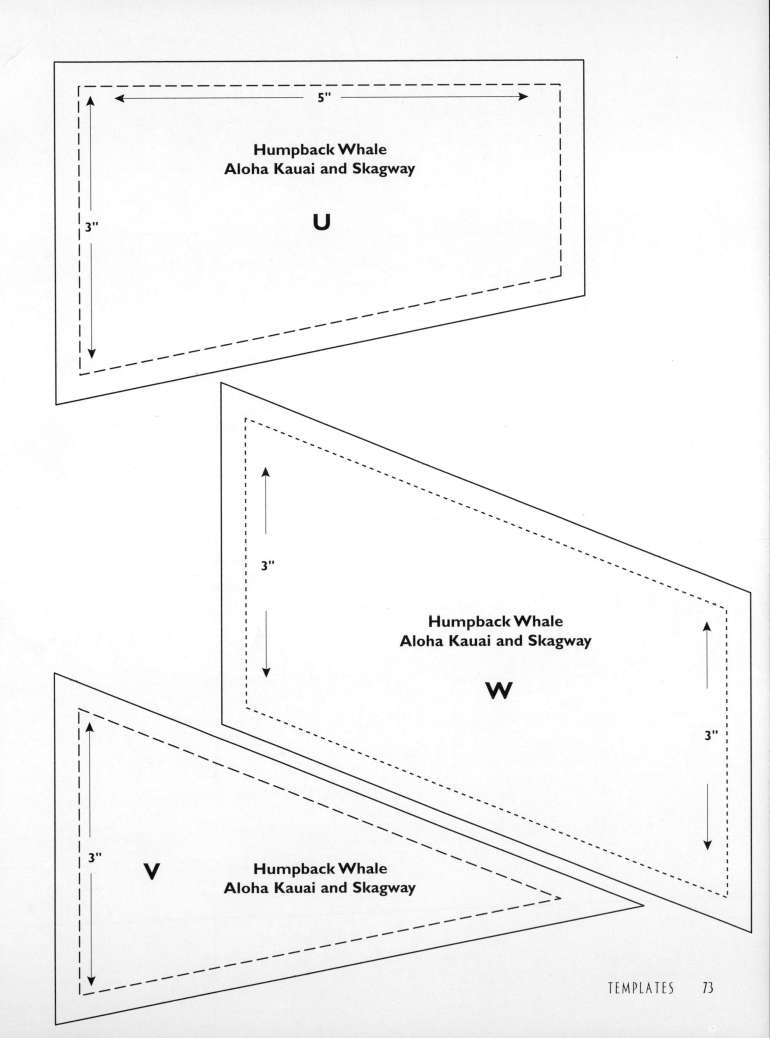

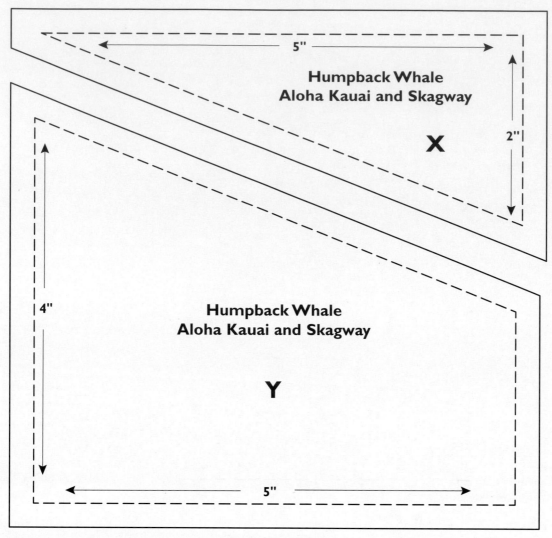

Humpback Whale
Aloha Kauai and Skagway

5"

2"

X

Humpback Whale
Aloha Kauai and Skagway

4"

5"

Y

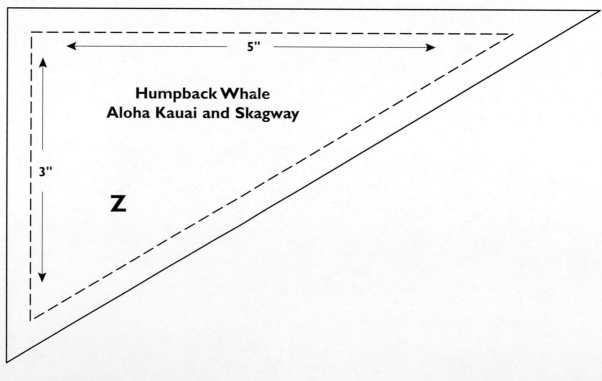

5"

Humpback Whale
Aloha Kauai and Skagway

3"

Z

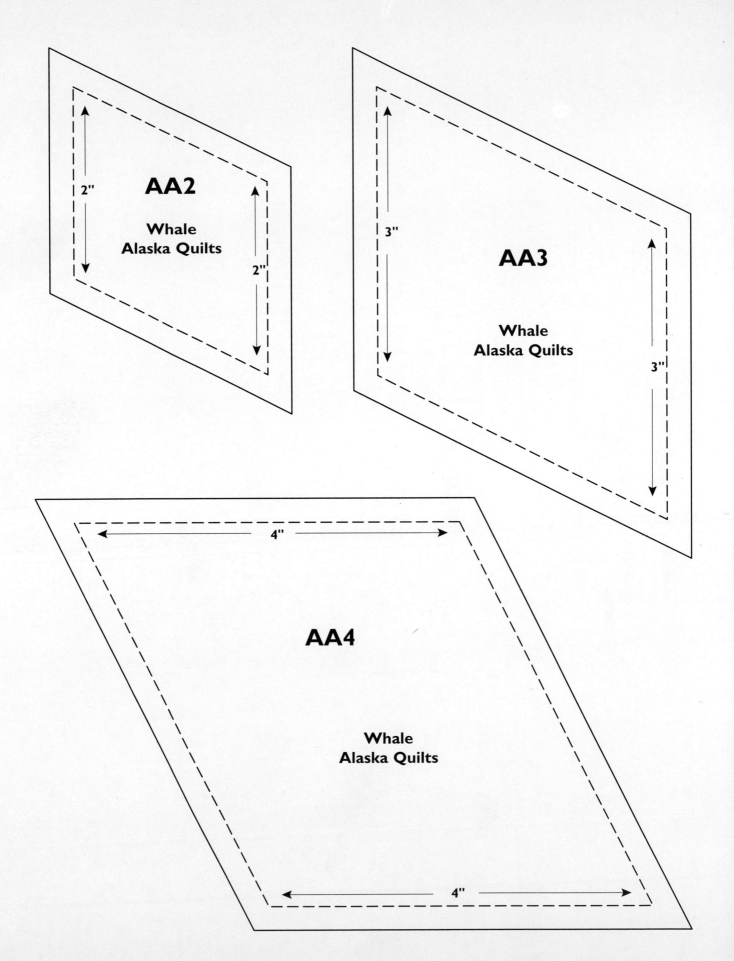

AA2

Whale
Alaska Quilts

2"

2"

AA3

Whale
Alaska Quilts

3"

3"

AA4

Whale
Alaska Quilts

4"

4"

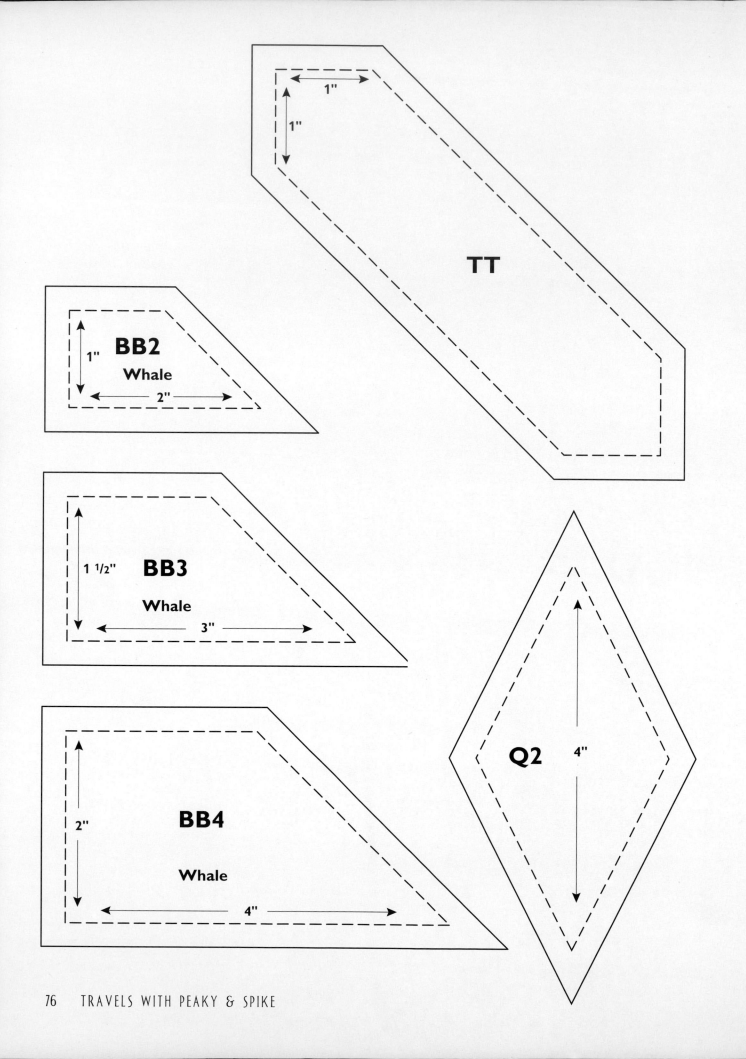

TT

BB2
Whale
1"
2"

BB3
Whale
1 1/2"
3"

BB4
Whale
2"
4"

Q2
4"

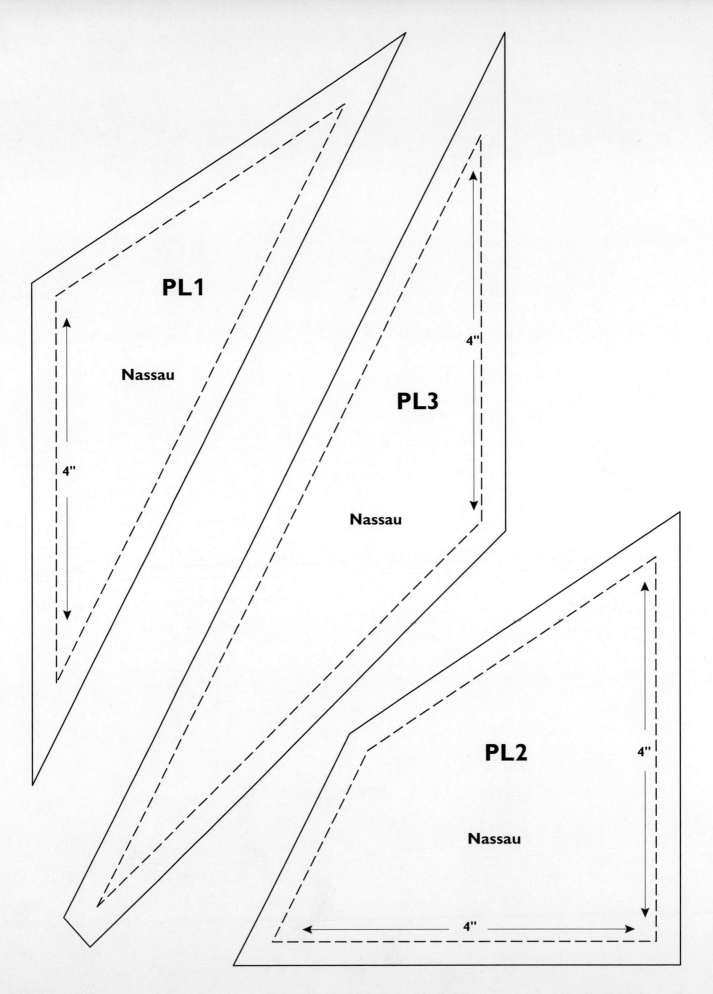

PL1

Nassau

4"

PL3

4"

Nassau

PL2

4"

Nassau

4"

About the Author

Doreen Speckmann, a beloved quilt teacher, designer, and author, passed away suddenly while on a teaching trip to Ireland.

Everyone at C&T is saddened by this loss. Doreen was a wonderful teacher who was loved by quilters all over the world. Our thoughts and prayers are with her family.

C&T Publishing remembers Doreen as an enthusiastic, vibrant friend who lived life exuberantly. She touched many quilters with her colorful quilts, entertaining stories, and hilarious sense of humor.

Doreen Speckmann will be deeply missed by everyone in the quilting world.

Cards and donations should be sent to:

Doreen Speckmann Fund
c/o A-1 Specialty Tours
2701 Sunset Point Road
Clearwater, FL 33759

C&T Booklist

Other Fine Books From C&T Publishing:

Anatomy of a Doll: The Fabric Sculptor's Handbook,
    Susanna Oroyan
Art & Inspirations: Ruth B. McDowell, Ruth B. McDowell
At Home with Patrick Lose: Colorful Quilted Projects,
    Patrick Lose
Color From the Heart: Seven Great Ways to Make Quilts with
    Colors You Love, Gai Perry
Crazy with Cotton, Diana Leone
Curves in Motion: Quilt Designs & Techniques, Judy B. Dales
Deidre Scherer: Work in Fabric & Thread, Deidre Scherer
Designing the Doll: From Concept to Construction,
    Susanna Oroyan
Easy Pieces: Creative Color Play with Two Simple Blocks,
    Margaret Miller
Exploring Machine Trapunto: New Dimensions, Hari Walner
The Fabric Makes the Quilt, Roberta Horton
Freddy's House: Brilliant Color in Quilts, Freddy Moran
Kaleidoscopes & Quilts, Paula Nadelstern
The New England Quilt Museum Quilts: Featuring the Story
    of the Mill Girls. With Instructions for 5 Heirloom Quilts,
    Jennifer Gilbert
The Photo Transfer Handbook: Snap It, Print It, Stitch It!,
    Jean Ray Laury
Piecing: Expanding the Basics, Ruth B. McDowell
Rotary Cutting with Alex Anderson: Tips, Techniques, and
    Projects, Alex Anderson

Scrap Quilts: The Art of Making Do, Roberta Horton
Simply Stars: Quilts that Sparkle, Alex Anderson
Six Color World: Color, Cloth, Quilts & Wearables,
    Yvonne Porcella
Skydyes: A Visual Guide to Fabric Painting, Mickey Lawler
Soft-Edge Piecing, Jinny Beyer
Start Quilting with Alex Anderson: Six Projects for First-Time
    Quilters, Alex Anderson
Stripes in Quilts, Mary Mashuta
Through the Garden Gate: Quilters and Their Gardens,
    Jean and Valori Wells
Wildflowers: Designs for Appliqué & Quilting,
    Carol Armstrong
Women of Taste: A Collaboration Celebrating Quilt Artists and
    Chefs, Girls, Inc., Girls Incorporated®

Sources

Cotton Patch Mail Order

3504 Hall Lane, Dept. CTB.

Lafayette, CA 94549

http://www.quiltusa.com

e-mail: cottonpa@aol.com

(800) 835-4418

(925) 283-7883

For information on cruises and tours with Doreen Speckmann

A1 Specialty Tours

2701 Sunset Point Road

Clearwater, FL 33759

1-800-677-9412

727-796-7555

727-797-1477 fax

www.a1specialtytours.com

For Peaky & Spike & Friends Template Set

Quilting from the Heartland

111 East St.

Starbuck, MN 56381

1-800-637-2541

320-239-4049 fax

www.qheartland.com

For triangle paper

SPPS

4410 N. Rancho Dr. #165

Las Vegas, NV 89130

702-658-7988

702-658-7133 fax

www.quiltime.com

For more funfilled designs by Mary Jo Scandin

Serendipity

PO Box 311

Sister Bay, WI 54234

920-854-5099

Thank Yous and Acknowledgments

Thanks—

to my mom and dad, David and Doris Punzel, for our interesting vacations and for letting me play with the sewing machine when I didn't know how;

to my daughter Megan for inspiring me to be a quilt-maker before she was born and for thinking I'm a cool mom twenty-two years later;

to Harold Nadel for making my words sound like me and keeping me on track;

to Mary Jo Scandin for drawing Peaky and Spike as I saw them in my head;

to Barb Kuhn and all the folks at C&T Publishing for their patience with an author who still has trouble getting everything together.

For more information write for a free catalog:
C&T Publishing, Inc.
P.O. Box 1456
Lafayette, CA 94549
(800) 284-1114
http://www.ctpub.com
e-mail: ctinfo@ctpub.com

Coming in Fall 2000

More Peaky and Spike patterns by Doreen Speckman will be available in Fall 2000 exclusively through the C&T web site - www.ctpub.com. If you are interested, send us an email (ctinfo@ctpub.com) and we will notify you via email when the patterns are available.

Index